MARILYN

AT TWENTIETH CENTURY FOX

MARI

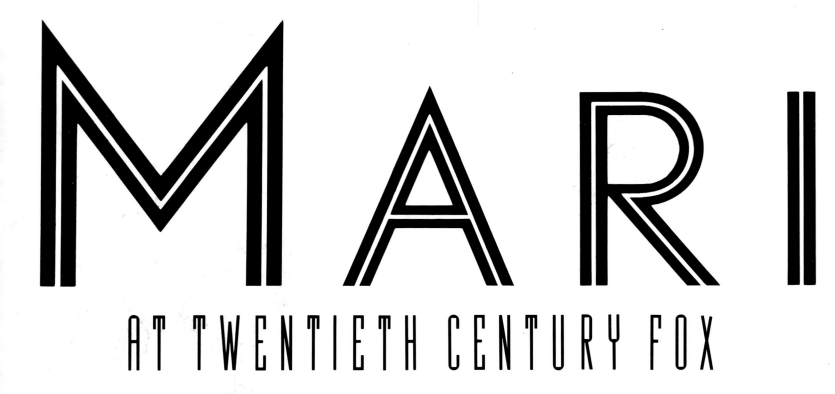

AT TWENTIETH CENTURY FOX

LAWRENCE CROWN

ZACHARY KWINTNER BOOKS LTD.

6 WARREN MEWS, LONDON W1P 5DJ

LYN

ACKNOWLEDGEMENTS

On a post-war summer day in 1946, a young photographer's model was put under
a standard starlet's contract to Twentieth Century Fox.
The studio's casting director helped her select a new name. And when she left the
sprawling lot on Pico Boulevard in West Los Angeles that day, Norma Jeane
Dougherty became Marilyn Monroe.
Without Fox, the studio for which she made twenty-one of her thirty films
(including her last picture, the never-completed 'Something's Got to Give'), there
might never have been a Marilyn Monroe. And without the cooperation of that
studio and the people listed alphabetically below, this book would not exist.

GENE ALLEN; CHUCK ASHMAN; JOHNNY CAMPBELL; ROY
CRAFT; NANCY CUSHING-JONES; MARVIN DAVIS;
MICHAEL FEILER, MD; JOE JASGUR; KEN KENYON; LIONEL
NEWMAN; RICHARD NEUHAUS; CHUCK PANAMA; MARTI
PIKE; JANE RUSSELL; WALTER SCOTT; ALLAN SNYDER;
MEG STAAHL; SONIA WOLFSON; PAUL WURTZEL; and *Pat
Miller*, for his assistance with the compilation of photographs; *Kimberley Wells*, for
editorial and research assistance; and numerous others who shared information and
offered help.

First published in 1987 by Planet Books, a division of
W.H. Allen & Co Plc

NOTE:

Designed by Osborn & Stephens Ltd

Typeset by Phoenix Photosetting Ltd, Chatham, Kent

Printed and bound in Singapore
for the publishers Zachary Kwintner Books Ltd
6 Warren Mews, London W1P 5DJ
ISBN 1 872532 04 7

NOTE:
Some of the photographs and illustrations in this book are not ideally suited to modern printing
techniques, but they have nevertheless been included because of their archival interest, which
the publishers feel should take precedence over quality of reproduction.

OPPOSITE: Marilyn during her early starlet days.
Courtesy Marc Wanamaker/The Bison Archives
Copyright © Twentieth Century Fox Film Corporation

Twentieth Century-Fox Film Corporation

STUDIOS
BEVERLY HILLS, CALIFORNIA   February 6, 1947

Miss Marilyn Monroe
c/o National Concert & Artists Corporation
9059 Sunset Blvd.
Los Angeles 46, California

Dear Miss Monroe:

This letter, when accepted by you, will confirm our mutual understanding and agreement, relative to the amendment of your contract of employment with us, dated August 24, 1946, as follows, but not otherwise:

It is mutually understood and agreed that Article Twenty-Fourth of your said contract of employment shall be and the same is hereby amended to read as follows:

"TWENTY-FOURTH: That all notices from the producer to the artist, under or in connection with this agreement, may be given in writing, by addressing the same to the artist in care of Elsie Cukor-Lipton Agency, 9157 Sunset Boulevard, Suite 301, Hollywood 46, California, and by depositing the same, so addressed, postage prepaid, in the United States mail, or at its option, the producer may deliver such notice to the artist personally, either orally or in writing. If such notice shall be sent by mail as above provided, the date of mailing shall be deemed to be the date of service of such notice."

All of the terms and conditions of your aforementioned contract of employment with us shall remain in full force and effect, except as herein specifically modified.

If the foregoing is in accordance with your understanding of our agreement, kindly execute this letter in quadruplicate by affixing your signature under the word "Accepted" at the end hereof, return three of said executed copies to us and retain the other for your records.

Form Approved
20th Century
Fox Film Corp.
Legal Department
Date 2/19/47

Yours very truly,

TWENTIETH CENTURY-FOX FILM CORPORATION

By

Its Executive Manager

ACCEPTED:

ABOVE: Letter of amendment to Marilyn Monroe's contract of employment with the Twentieth Century Fox Film Corporation*. Note that below the Marilyn signature is the handwritten 'Norma Jeane Dougherty'.

Copyright © Twentieth Century Fox Film Corporation

* Note: In 1984, the Twentieth Century Fox Film Corporation removed the hyphen in its name. The text of this book follows the current correct usage.

CONTENTS

Marilyn Monroe's Fox Films

1948
SCUDDA HOO! SCUDDA HAY!
■

Marilyn's first role was in this boy-meets-recalcitrant-mules romantic comedy. She was cut out of the picture.

1948
DANGEROUS YEARS
■

A cautionary melodrama about hoods and juvenile delinquents. Marilyn was a waitress at the local teenage hangout.

1950
TICKET TO TOMAHAWK
■

A Western in which a group of travelling showgirls are caught in the battle between a railroad and a stagecoach line for the Tomahawk, Colorado charter. Marilyn was one of the chorus girls and did a song-and-dance number with Dan Dailey.

1950
ALL ABOUT EVE
■

Monroe caught the attention of studio executives, critics and the public in her minor role as the blonde on George Sanders' arm in this acclaimed backstage-Broadway tale.

1950
THE FIREBALL
■

Orphan Mickey Rooney has to overcome the inner perils of success before he becomes a true rollerskating champion. Marilyn played one of Mickey's distractions on his way to the top and to true love.

1951
AS YOUNG AS YOU FEEL
■

Marilyn was the boss's secretary in this comedy about a man who impersonates the visiting company president when he is forced to retire.

1951
LOVE NEST
■

A soldier returns from the war to find his wife has spent their savings on a rickety boarding house in New York. He invites his old army buddy 'Bobby' (Monroe) to rent a room just as the FBI arrives to investigate another tenant. All ends happily. (Oddly enough, this picture was originally called 'A Wac in his Life' when the Marilyn part was at best a second subplot.)

1951
LET'S MAKE IT LEGAL
▪

On the eve of her divorce, Claudette Colbert is courted by a wealthy former suitor, much to her ex-husband's dismay. Marilyn was the young model eager to court the wealthy suitor herself.

1952
WE'RE NOT MARRIED
▪

Five couples discover their marriages aren't legal. Husband David Wayne is upset that Marilyn is spending all her time competing to become Mrs America instead of staying home with him. When she discovers she isn't really married, she goes after the *Miss* America title. In the end, she opts for a second marriage to Wayne. Marilyn was heavily featured in the picture's advertising campaign.

1952
DON'T BOTHER TO KNOCK
▪

Marilyn's first dramatic starring role was a psychotic babysitter, for whom Richard Widmark falls.

1952
MONKEY BUSINESS
▪

Marilyn played a sexy secretary again in this Cary Grant–Ginger Rogers comedy, in which Grant is a somewhat pixilated scientist who accidentally swallows a youth elixir.

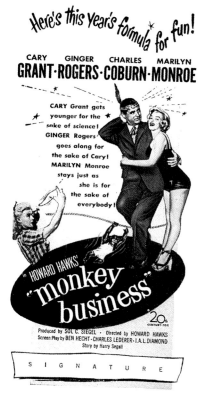

1952
O. HENRY'S FULL HOUSE
▪

In the classic story, Charles Laughton is the bum trying to get arrested so he can winter in a warm jail; she is the streetwalker he encounters.

1953
NIAGARA
▪

Marilyn plots to kill husband Joseph Cotton on their honeymoon at Niagara Falls. This *film noire* melodrama was a star vehicle for Marilyn, who also sang one Lionel Newman song before her character got her just desserts.

Continued overleaf

for sheer power... for sheer magnetism... the show **Marilyn Monroe** puts on is as electric and spectacular as *Niagara* itself!

2Oth Century-Fox presents

STARRING
MARILYN MONROE · JOSEPH COTTEN · JEAN PETERS
COLOR BY *Technicolor*

Marilyn Monroe's Fox Films

1953
HOW TO MARRY A MILLIONAIRE
▪

Monroe, Grable and Bacall rent a penthouse apartment to attract millionaire husbands.

1955
SEVEN YEAR ITCH
▪

A lonely married businessman fantasizes about the model who lives upstairs in his New York apartment building. This picture featured the billowing-skirt scene that became an icon in the public's imagination.

1953
GENTLEMEN PREFER BLONDES
▪

Marilyn and Jane Russell co-starred in this romantic musical comedy set partly aboard the luxury ocean liner *Ile de France*. 'Diamonds Are A Girl's Best Friend' was Marilyn's show-stopping number. The public and studio executives alike were amazed by her singing and dancing abilities.

1954
RIVER OF NO RETURN
▪

Marilyn is a saloon singer who joins Robert Mitchum and his son on a dangerous river raft journey to escape the Indians. Her Lionel Newman–Ken Darby songs included 'One Silver Dollar' and the title song.

1954
THERE'S NO BUSINESS LIKE SHOW BUSINESS
▪

Marilyn played the Broadway-bound hat-check girl who joins the act of a vaudeville family led by Ethel Merman and Dan Dailey. She falls for son Donald O'Connor. Marilyn's big solo number was 'Heat Wave'.

1962
SOMETHING'S GOT TO GIVE
■

Lost in a shipwreck, Marilyn finally is rescued years later only to discover that her husband has remarried. This is the film Marilyn never finished.

1956
BUS STOP
■

A lonesome cowboy kidnaps a second-rate saloon singer, planning to force her to marry him. They are trapped in a bus-stop café when the roads are blocked.

1960
LET'S MAKE LOVE
■

Millionaire Yves Montand tries to stop an off-Broadway show from spoofing him . . . until he sees Marilyn performing in it. When Montand's identity is mistaken, he is hired to perform in the show, and in turn he hires Milton Berle and Gene Kelly (playing themselves) to teach him how to perform.

NON-FOX FILMS

'Ladies of the Chorus' (1948)
'Love Happy' (1950)
'The Asphalt Jungle' (1950)
'Right Cross' (1950)
'Hometown Story' (1951)
'Clash by Night' (1952)
'The Prince and the Showgirl' (1957)
'Some Like It Hot' (1959)
'The Misfits' (1961)

ℐntroduction

For millions of people all over the world, Marilyn Monroe *was* the movies. Time has not diminished her legend.

Between 1948 and 1962, she appeared in thirty films. Both her first picture, in which her scenes ended up on the cutting room floor, and her last, which was never completed, were for Twentieth Century Fox. Nineteen other films were completed for the studio at which she spent some of her happiest – and most troubled – days.

In 'Scudda Hoo! Scudda Hay!', the less than memorable story of a country boy and his mules, Marilyn was one of two girls rowing a canoe on a lake. Her big scene (reproduced overleaf) was cut from the picture before its release.

In the few scenes she shot fourteen years later for 'Something's Got to Give', Marilyn was a luminous presence. A few short months after she posed for her glowing wardrobe tests (reproduced on page 186), she was dead – at the age of thirty-six.

Continued on page 17

RIGHT: Marilyn and Colleen Townsend during a rehearsal of 'Scudda Hoo! Scudda Hay!'
Copyright © Twentieth Century Fox Film Corporation

LEFT: Cast and crew of 'Scudda Hoo! Scudda Hay!', the first film Marilyn Monroe worked on at Twentieth Century Fox: Marilyn in centre, with stars Lon McCallister and June Haver just below.
Copyright © Twentieth Century Fox Film Corporation

THIS PAGE AND OPPOSITE: Marilyn Monroe and Colleen
Townsend in cut scene from 'Scudda Hoo!
Scudda Hay!' Robert Karnes is the actor doing
a spot of fishing.

In the years since her death in August 1962, Marilyn's life has taken on the cosmic proportions of myth. The orphanage childhood that, to some, suggests Dickens-with-palm-trees; the meteoric rise from backlot 'stock kid starlet' to show-stopping sex goddess; the stormy love–hate relationships with her husbands and lovers, her colleagues and public, her studio and the press; and the controversy surrounding her death – all this is the stuff of legend.

It becomes all too easy to forget that Marilyn Monroe was a flesh-and-blood person who passed through the Fox front gate each morning when she arrived for work – all too often hours late – that she walked the studio streets and made movies in its cavernous sound stages. But it is impossible for the men and women who worked with her at Fox to forget.

LEFT: Fox film lot *circa* 1950.
Courtesy Marc Wanamaker/The Bison Film Archives
Copyright © Twentieth Century Fox Film Corporation

OPPOSITE PAGE: Marilyn on location during the filming of 'Scudda Hoo! Scudda Hay!'
Copyright © Twentieth Century Fox Film Corporation

A number of her one-time co-workers are still alive. Some still work at the studio. Many are fiercely protective of her memory and are eager to set the record straight. A few have never before spoken publicly:

Her personal make-up man – who did her first screen test and almost every one of her pictures, and who, years later, came at the request of Joe DiMaggio to make up her body for the funeral – recalls their long-time relationship . . .

The publicist who was Fox's 'Marilyn specialist' remembers a two a.m. mob scene caused by Marilyn's presence on a New York street, tells the truth behind her famous quips and reveals the ploys he used to combat her tardiness . . .

A six-time Academy Award-winning art and set decorator, whose Hollywood career spans half a century, compares Marilyn to the other stars he knew and worked with over the years . . .

The special effects specialist who controlled the wind machine under the subway grate in the famous billowing-skirt scene tells what it was like on the set of 'The Seven Year Itch' and recalls shooting arrows at Marilyn on location for 'River of No Return'.

But before they and others tell their stories and the stories of her films,

there is a Hollywood girl's life to remember and the history of a major motion-picture studio to tell.

Should we be surprised that there is so little agreement about the basic facts of her early life?

After all, she was a native Hollywood girl (born 1 June, 1926), from the outskirts of a city where turning fiction into reality (and vice versa) is the central industry, and where armies of press agents are employed to rewrite the past – if need be – to suit the needs of the present.

Add to this the biographical details that were deemed unacceptable to the public in the puritanical late 1940s and early '50s – such as her mother's mental illness, the famous nude calendar pose, her own supposed illegitimacy (although, according to documents discovered after her father's death, her parents had been married at her birth and only divorced later) and even the correct spelling of her given name (it was 'Norma Jean*e*' on her birth certificate), as well as her own life-long monumental insecurities, and it shouldn't be surprising that Marilyn, while still only a starlet, almost turned down her first substantive feature story in a national magazine because she was afraid her true story would be made public. (Her studio publicist recalls that she went through with the 1951 interview only after he convinced her that the magazine's reporters weren't 'out to get her' and could be trusted to sanitize the facts. For years afterwards, her mother was referred to only as 'an invalid', and Marilyn's succession of foster homes became 'the aunts and uncles who raised her'.)

From shortly after Marilyn's birth, her mother was confined in various mental institutions for what probably was congenital manic-depression. Marilyn's maternal grandparents also were hospitalized in mental institutions and an uncle committed suicide. Throughout her life – Marilyn confided to friends on a number of occasions – she feared her family's tendency toward mental illness might have been passed to her and would be passed on if she had children of her own.

'To me, she was just that red-headed woman,' Marilyn was reported to have said of her mother. The ambivalence is not surprising given that she spent her childhood in a Hollywood orphanage and in a dozen different foster homes – including, on separate occasions, those of a religious zealot and of a group of English acrobats who had come to Hollywood to break into the movies.

At sixteen, young Norma Jeane married for the first time. In one of those real-life coincidences that are all the more incredible for being true, actress Jane Russell, who years later would co-star with Marilyn Monroe in 'Gentlemen Prefer Blondes', recalls a chance meeting with a former Van Nuys, California, classmate, Jim Dougherty:

'We were at a dance someplace. Jim was dancing with her. They were on the floor and he looked over and said, "I want you to meet my wife." And I just waved and she waved back.'

And so passed the first, improbable meeting between the two young women – still unknown Southern California teenagers – who one day would be *the* Jane Russell and *the* Marilyn Monroe.

Jane and Marilyn's first husband are friends to this day, but Jane and Marilyn never again spoke to each other about that brief meeting.

When Norma Jeane accepted the marriage proposal of Jane Russell's high-school friend Jim, he was an aircraft worker and she was living with an aunt whom she loved. Sources differ on the reasons she accepted handsome Jim Dougherty's proposal:

Was it because her beloved aunt was dying, or was it because her uncle was making advances towards the beautiful teenager? Or was it, simply, young love for the boy next door?

At any rate, she went off to work at the aircraft plant and her new husband went off to war. It was at the plant that an army photographer discovered her and she realized her natural affinity for the camera.

RIGHT AND OPPOSITE PAGE: Marilyn had a natural affinity with the camera as these early pictures clearly demonstrate.

Her picture was sent overseas, and the Seventh Division Medical Corps voted her the girl they would most like to examine. Soon, Norma Jeane was spending more time in photographers' studios than on the assembly line.

'I wasn't exactly a fool,' she told a reporter in the early 1950s. 'I was aware I was attractive to men. The fellows (at the aircraft plant) used to whistle at me and one time the foreman moved me behind a partition so I wouldn't distract the men.'

From that first photograph on, the story has the aura of inevitability: from photographer's subject to professional model; from modelling agency to talent agency; from talent agency to film studio; and, at the age of twenty, newly divorced, through the gates of Twentieth Century Fox.

'Kiss me, my fool!' read the most famous title card in the 1918 silent film that created William Fox's first internationally known female star – the exotic Theda Bara.

Fox was a Hollywood pioneer. In 1935, his Fox Film Corporation merged with 20th Century Pictures to create the present film studio, which in 1981 was purchased by Denver oil magnate Marvin Davis, who later sold it to its present owner, publishing magnate Rupert Murdoch.

From the silent era onward, female stars played an especially big part in the history of Twentieth Century Fox. First was smouldering vamp Theda Bara herself, but after her came such beauties as Loretta Young, Constance Bennett, Janet Gaynor, Alice Faye, Anne Baxter, Susan Hayward, Jennifer Jones, Gene Tierney, Sonja Henie, Jeanne Crain, Vivian Blaine and June Haver.

In the 1930s and '40s, the studio was home to America's two favourite blondes. In the '30s it was America's sweetheart, Shirley Temple; and in the '40s it was the doughboys' favourite pin-up, Betty Grable.

From William Fox's time on, the studio was run by a succession of shrewd showmen. From the mid '30s to the mid '50s, Darryl Zanuck headed Fox, and it is generally believed that he turned the necessity of keeping his greatest female stars' contract demands under control into a virtue by keeping on the lot a 'pool' of starlets who were available to replace a too-demanding actress. If, for example, a Betty Grable's demands became too great, another young blonde beauty always could be groomed – and in fact already was on the lot – to replace her.

When young Marilyn first was put under contract, Grable was the studio's reigning star. Whether or not Darryl Zanuck saw Marilyn's screen test and immediately thought of her as a potential successor, no one can say. What is certain is that under the old studio system then in effect, no starlet could have ascended to the firmament without years of innumerable bit parts and countless promotional appearances. And in the period before she became a megastar, the studio once almost gave her up to its cross-town rival.

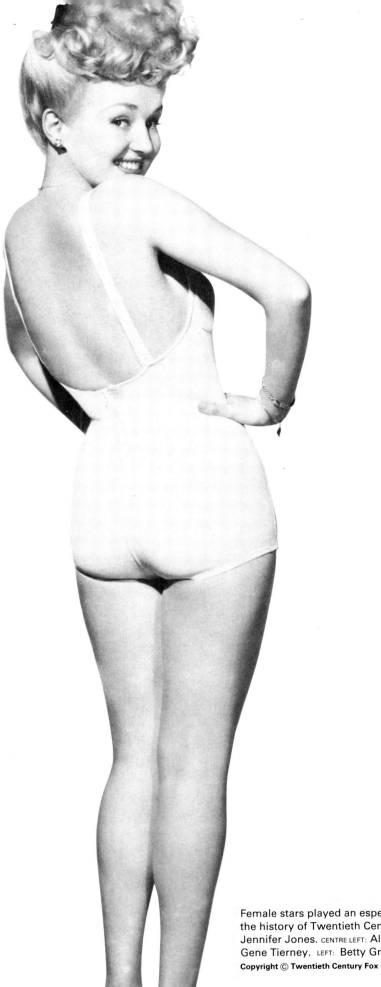

Female stars played an especially big part in the history of Twentieth Century Fox. TOP: Jennifer Jones. CENTRE LEFT: Alice Faye. BOTTOM LEFT: Gene Tierney. LEFT: Betty Grable.

ABOVE: One of Marilyn's many promotional
appearances, without which neither she nor
any other starlet could hope to rise to stardom.
Courtesy Marc Wanamaker/The Bison Archives
Copyright © Twentieth Century Fox Film Corporation

Stock Kid/Starlet

Hollywood was approaching mid-century. Tinseltown's Golden Age was ending and few could see that a new one would follow the long decline of the 1950s that was then just beginning. Audiences – mesmerized by the brand-new home screen of television – were deserting theatres in droves. (Today, a studio may make as much, or more, from its teleproduction division as it makes from its feature-film division. Then, there were no television divisions at the studios, and the small screen was regarded as the enemy.) Attendance figures, box-office receipts and, most important of all, profits, were all declining. Studio chiefs were anxious for *something* – whether a new technical process like CinemaScope or a compelling new star – to hold audiences.

The entrenched studio star system still was in full swing, with each of the powerful Hollywood dream factories grooming its own stable of stars. Talented hopefuls by the score were 'optioned', under stock contracts, by the studios. The stock contracts rarely paid well and the 'stock kids', as they were called, rarely rose above the level of chorus boy or girl in the background of a musical or – if they were lucky – a bit part with a few lines of dialogue.

Between the real and aspiring stars and their public were the gossip columns and the fan magazines. In those days, the studios kept scores and scores of press agents on staff – in the case of Fox, its approximately ninety-person publicity department was the equivalent of the city room of the largest of metropolitan newspapers; the publicists' job was not only to mould public opinion, but to mediate between the all-powerful columnists and the actors and actresses on contract to the studio.

The power the columnists and the magazines wielded is hard to imagine today: Hedda Hopper and Louella Parsons; Walter Winchell and Sidney Skolsky; they and a few others like them, and the magazines like *Photoplay*, could break – or make – entire careers.

Allan 'Whitey' Snyder – one of Hollywood's premier make-up artists – was with Marilyn Monroe both at the beginning and at the end. He generally is recognized as having been one of her closest confidants, one of the very few working people on the sets of her films to make the transition to close, personal friend. As one studio executive put it, 'Stars only confide in two people – their wardrobe mistress and their make-up man. That's because they're the two people the star spends the most time with.' Whitey was her make-up man; his wife once was Marilyn's wardrobe mistress.

Whitey had already been working in the movie business for a decade when he first met Marilyn. He had started out in 1937 as a studio messenger, making $15 per week, but was persuaded to move to the make-up department at RKO by the prospect of a $5-per-week raise. In 1942, he moved to Fox.

Whitey has worked on 345 feature films and more than 400 television shows in his long and distinguished career. He made Marilyn up for her first Fox screen test, but 'didn't do much' for her because 'she wasn't big enough' for a man who was then making-up stars like Betty Grable and Gene Tierney.

Whitey remembers that Marilyn . . .

'. . . brought with her a lot of strange ideas about how to do make-up. She had outlandish make-up: she wanted her chin out; she wanted her nose shaded . . .

'I was there but she didn't let me touch her. She did it herself like a clown.

'(Leon) Shamroy, the cinematographer, and I got up on the test stage and he said, "What the hell is that? Did you do that, Whitey?"

'I didn't know what to say and she said, "No, I did it."

'So he said, "Go back to the make-up department, wash your face and let him do it right."

'(This time) I did the same things she wanted, but blended them in and helped her out in a way she didn't know how to do. We worked together from then on and improved her make-up as we went along year after year.'

From then on, Marilyn wanted Whitey to be her make-up man. And even in those early years, when she was only getting stock-kid chorus parts, he obliged whenever he was available.

In later years, did she continue to trust him because he had helped even when she was an unknown? Was it because his professional skill brought out her own imperfect vision of herself and her potential for glamour?

Whitey himself offers two reasons. First, he was known throughout the industry for his speed – no small advantage when it came to working with someone like Marilyn who – from the earliest days of her budding career – was habitually tardy for appointments of all kinds. Whitey could do Marilyn's make-up in twenty minutes versus the two hours it took others.

And second, 'she trusted me; I wasn't on the make for her.'

June Haver and Vivian Blaine were two young actresses that made it out from the stock-ghetto, Whitey recalls. But they, and Marilyn, were exceptions. Whitey remembers that back in those days . . .

'Fox had about 70 girls and 70 guys under contract – what they used to call the "stable" – and a lot of the time they used to use those gals and guys in the background of musicals . . . very seldom would they give them a part that was worth anything. They had this (standard stock) contract that went from seventy-five to fifteen hundred (dollars per week) . . . After six months (the studio) would say, "If you want to stay on at the same (low) salary, you can." And they all would. Only one or two people ever graduated out of that thing.'

At first, it didn't seem that Marilyn would be one of them. Fox, the studio that had discovered her, didn't pick up the second option on her stock contract.

Marilyn had been in two pictures. In the first, 'Scudda Hoo', her entire part was excised; in the second, 'Dangerous Years' (produced by film pioneer Sol Wurtzel), she had a bit part as a waitress in a soda shop. Although she had fewer than ten lines of dialogue (her longest single line: '*And now you're blowing it on two Cokes*'), her fresh, luminous-blonde presence fairly lit up the screen. Nonetheless, it wasn't enough to save her from the unemployment line.

After several months of unemployment, Marilyn (thanks at least in part to the intercession of powerful Fox executive producer Joe Schenk) had *another* stock contract, this time for the Columbia Pictures of legendary movie mogul Harry Cohn. It was at Columbia that Marilyn met Natasha Lytess, one of the drama coaches who was to wield extraordinary – some would say Svengali-like – influence over her.

After six months and another bit part, Columbia, too, declined to pick up the option on Marilyn's contract and it was back to odd jobs, making the rounds at the studios and unemployment.

During this, the lowest ebb in her career, Marilyn posed for the famous nude calendar picture known as 'Golden Dreams'. Despite the film parts to her credit, she was broke. Marilyn herself described the circumstances (in an article 'by Marilyn Monroe *as told to* Liza Wilson' that appeared in *American Weekly*, 23 November, 1952):

'I got four weeks behind in my rent at the Studio Club (in Hollywood) and the manager – she had been most kind and patient – finally had to tell me to pay up or move on.

'Nearly every photographer I had ever worked with had asked me to pose in the nude. But I had always refused.

'One photographer, Tom Kelley, I liked very much. I had done some beer ads for Tom and his wife, Natalie, and they asked me if I would like to do a nude for a calendar firm. They said no one would recognize me. I refused at first.

'But the day I received my eviction notice I called Natalie and said, "When and how much?"

'They arranged for me to pose at the studio that night. I received $50. The next day I paid my rent and treated myself to a quiet dinner at home.'

Marilyn wasn't under studio contract for her next picture, 'Ticket to Tomahawk', a musical spoof of Westerns released in 1950, but she was back at Fox.

Again, she had no dialogue (according to Marilyn in the *Weekly* article, 'I didn't even say "hello" in this – just "hummmmm"').

Still, on location in the isolated Rocky mountains, she did attract the attention of the picture's co-star, Anne Baxter, who in her autobiography, *Intermission* (G. P. Putnam, 1976), takes a disapproving tone about the bit player who played one of the chorus girls:

'Marilyn Monroe came in with a different crew member every night, wearing the same sweater. She was eminently braless and I particularly remember the pink V-necked angora sweater. It was said she slept in it. We never saw hide nor hair of her, or of her two roommates, outside of dinnertime or during their occasional days of shooting. They slept whenever possible and all day Sunday. Or they were closeted in the only phone booth, calling Hollywood.'

From her earliest days in films, Marilyn Monroe was a study in contradictions and paradoxes. Was she promiscuous or was she a sexual innocent? Did the studio use her or was 'Marilyn Monroe' her own conscious creation, an act she turned on and off at will for the benefit of the camera and her public? Was she a naif or was she herself shrewder than the wiliest Hollywood publicist? Even those who knew her best are not in complete agreement.

BELOW: Marilyn at right in the chorus line of 'Ticket to Tomahawk'.

Former Fox publicist John Campbell, for example, remembers her as . . .

'. . . a stock girl who hung around the publicity department all the time. I was what they called a "planter"; I was the primary contact between the press and the publicity operation. She'd come into the office in her tight sweater and just hang around. And I so often wished she'd go away – she was friendly and there was no point in being rude to her. Then cut to her final picture – I couldn't get within thirty feet of her . . . Like so many things in life, it came full circle: I wanted to get rid of her and she *did* get rid of me.'

The stock girl in the tight sweater was a willing volunteer for studio publicity assignments, Campbell recalls:

'She was one of those gals who would always cut a ribbon for you to open a new supermarket or something. She was very useful in that regard.'

Moving from stock-kid to starlet status, Marilyn was 'very eager for publicity', agrees Roy Craft, who since 1958 has been a rural Washington state 'country newspaperman'. But in the early 1950s, Craft was a Fox publicist and, for the first five years of her stardom – her 'happy years', as he calls them – Craft was the studio's 'Marilyn expert'. He says: '. . . I just got to be by a sort of custom – by a process of osmosis – the Marilyn expert.'

Craft started out as a publicity 'unit man', who worked with photographers on 'pretty girl pictures'. With Marilyn . . .

'. . . I was trying to get more outdoor-type pretty-girl shots, at the beach on the sand, as distinguished from the old studio pin-up with the bearskin rug and against the pillar and so on.' Craft remembers that the major gossip columnists of the era – Hedda Hopper and Louella Parsons – paid Marilyn no attention until she had reached full-fledged sex-symbol status:

ABOVE AND OVERLEAF: These 'beach' photos were taken on the Fox lot.
Courtesy of Roy Craft

'Her build-up was sort of in reverse to the normal, sort of an upside-down pyramid. A lot of the youngsters in Hollywood will start with local publicity and work their way up and eventually they make the cover of a major national magazine. Marilyn started at the top and finally worked her way until she was mentioned in the local gossip column.'

Craft, who had worked at *Life* magazine before he came to Fox, had got Marilyn cover photos in *Life* and *Look* magazines before *Colliers* finally expressed an interest in doing a 'profile-type' story. But publicity-eager Marilyn balked . . .

'*Colliers* people wanted to do a real story on her (as opposed to a simple picture-with-caption) . . . I went up and had a cocktail with her at Mocambo or one of those places on the (Sunset) Strip – incidentally, she wasn't a drinker in those days; she nursed a Dacquiri or something while I had a few belts.
'I said, "Marilyn, *Colliers* wants to do a story on you, but it will be what we call a profile, or an in-depth story. Up 'till now, you've been a name going with a pretty picture. If they do this story," I said, "they'll want to go into detail on your life, where you've been and what you've done and so forth."
'And she said, "Well, if your mother was crazy and you never knew who your father was, what would you say?"
'I said, "For openers, you'd tell the truth. These people aren't out to crucify you. Illegitimacy is not something they're going to play with. We'll explain your background and that your mother is a mental invalid and just suggest they be good enough to say your mother was an invalid and your father died before you were born.'

'This was the story which they all accepted and which they all went along with until she got to be so big that (reporter) Ilene Mosby broke the story of her mother being in a hospital . . .

Meantime, *Colliers* finally did do the story.'

An early *Colliers* story described a backlot incident from the young starlet's career that may have been apocryphal or, if not, was almost certainly staged:

'One March day the publicity department set up a shot in which she posed clad in a flesh-coloured negligée. Afterwards she had to walk a quarter mile back to the wardrobe department to get her clothes, and a strong wind had arisen as she strolled up the company street past the administration building. Word of what was happening passed around like lightning.
' "It was like the Lindbergh home-coming," recalls one studio executive. "People were leaning out of every window. And there was Marilyn, naïve and completely unperturbed, smiling and waving up at everybody she knew, didn't know or hoped to know." '

Marilyn's next big break came outside the Fox lot. Her new and influential agent, Johnny Hyde, helped her get a small but important part in John Huston's 'The Asphalt Jungle'.
Not only did the critics and the public notice her, but so did writer/director Joseph Mankiewicz who was then preparing to film – with a stellar cast – a backstage look at life on Broadway.
The picture was 'All About Eve', and as a result of her role in it, Marilyn was signed to a seven-year contract at Fox. From this point on, the studio's star-making machine was clearly working on her behalf. But as a number of those most closely connected to her in that period have declared, Marilyn Monroe's best publicist was herself.

OVERLEAF: Did one of these cause an on-lot sensation?

All About Eve/All About Marilyn

'That was the picture that turned things around for her,' remembers six-time Academy Award-winning art and set decorator Walter Scott, who garnered the first of his twenty-two Oscar nominations for his work on 'Eve'.

In the heady period during and immediately after that production, Marilyn's former Columbia drama coach, Natasha Lytess, resigned from her job at that studio to work full-time with Marilyn, and Marilyn signed her new long-term contract with Fox.

Marilyn's sudden public prominence was mirrored by an equally sudden in-studio prominence. Issue after issue of the Fox in-house magazine, *Action*, featured Marilyn Monroe.

Once again, the part that won Marilyn all this attention was miniscule. She played Miss Caswell, ambitious young protégée of powerful New York theatre critic Addison DeWitt (played by George Sanders), on whose arm she arrives at a party attended by Eve (Anne Baxter) and Margo (Bette Davis).

In Joseph Mankiewicz's 1949 'treatment' for the script that later became 'All About Eve', Marilyn's entire part flashes by in less than a page. The scene is a theatre-people party, where the conversation has turned as bitchy as the guests:

OPPOSITE: Cover of ACTION magazine, dated April 1951, showing Marilyn reflected in sunglasses.
Copyright © Twentieth Century Fox Film Corporation

'Addison (Sanders) is just arriving with Miss Caswell (Monroe). Margo (Davis) takes another martini from a passing waiter before greeting him. She calls Miss Caswell, Miss Brody – Addison reminds her that was last month. He upbraids Margo for giving the party – he had always hoped that she, like he, had no friends – and assured her his only reason for coming was to enable her to make it a tax deduction.

'Eve (Baxter) comes down the stairs. She greets Addison with due deference. Margo is surprised they've met. "Here and there," says Addison, "in passing." Margo suggests they have a nice long talk – Eve is so interested in the theatre. Addison is all for it; Eve hopes she won't bore him. Miss Caswell (Monroe) opens her beautiful kisser. "Not only won't you bore him, honey," she says, "you won't even get to talk." Addison turns an icy smile on Miss Caswell. He points out Max. "That little man is Max Fabian. He is a producer. You are lost at sea and he is a lighthouse. You are dying of thirst on a desert and he is a water hole. Go do yourself some good." Miss Caswell sighs. "Why do they always look like unhappy rabbits?" "Because that's what they are," says Addison, "Go make him happy." Miss Caswell goes . . .'

Miss Caswell's departure marked Marilyn Monroe's arrival. 'Eve' was named Best Picture of 1950.

Continued on page 42

THE COVER

Photo by Pashkousky.

Paul Piper, Mail department, has no trouble portraying the old saying about spring being the time when a young man's fancy turns to thoughts of beautiful girls. Who should he be focusing his eyes upon other than luscious Marilyn Monroe, shapely 20th Century-Fox actress. Piper was responsible for the recent and successful Studio Club little theater venture, "Ah, Wilderness," the three acter which was acclaimed by a packed house for almost a week. In addition to the taxing director's chores, Paul carried a strong leading part. However, a close observati... cover will reve... didn't need an... prompting with... blonde in front of h...

On The Side

APRIL'S COVER

We thought last month's Action was going to be a perfect issue. All was peaceful. Then a week after the magazine was mailed, we received a deluge of threats because the luscious cover girl, Marilyn Monroe, was so small everyone had red rimmed eyes from squinting.

Graduating from Van Nuys High School, shapely Jane Russell's Alma Mater, Marilyn is destined to film stardom like Mrs. Bob Waterfield.

Like many of the young, modern and ambitious actresses, Marilyn started in school plays and later filled in as a part time model. The curvy blonde's first picture at Twentieth was "Scudda Hoo, Scudda Hay." Her face went the traditional rounds of Hollywood's cutting room floors till she clicked in MGM's "Asphalt Jungle." That led to a snappy part in Zanuck's "All About Eve," and she recently completed "Will You Love Me In December."

But why waste your time with these facts; here's what you want below.

MARILYN MONROE

ABOVE: Publicity still from 'All About Eve'. Left to
right: Anne Baxter, Bette Davis, Marilyn
Monroe, George Sanders.
Copyright © Twentieth Century Fox Film Corporation

Writer/director Joseph Mankiewicz won Oscars for Direction and Screenplay, and George Sanders won as Best Supporting Actor. Edith Head and Charles LeMaire also shared an 'Eve' Oscar for Best Costume Design (for a black-and-white picture).

Former publicist Roy Craft, too, remembers 'Eve' as the turning point in Marilyn's career:

'"Asphalt Jungle" had been very important because she had attracted some attention, but it was in "Eve" that we began getting publicity for Marilyn as distinguished from just another starlet cutting ribbons in a supermarket. It was in "Eve" that we really started working with her.'

A number of observers have remarked on how starstruck the young Marilyn seemed on the set of 'Eve'. Walter Scott puts it this way:

'She was in awe of Bette Davis when she was making "All About Eve". She was nervous when she was in the company of someone like Celeste Holm or Bette Davis.'

Scott goes on to make the point that, while she may not have fully comprehended the implications of her own subsequent stardom, Marilyn was highly conscious of the star status of others:

'I think the record will show she was not late with Mankiewicz on "All About Eve", and she wasn't late when she was playing with all these important stars on "There's No Business Like Show Business" (1954) . . . She didn't hold up those companies like she did some others.

'I think if she was sufficiently awed – by (Ethel) Merman or someone like that–

she was conscious of the fact that she wanted to be liked by these important people.

'She didn't want a reigning star to say, "Oh, that little thing, she held us all up." I'm sure she was conscious of that.'

Roy Craft, though, recalls the famous allusion to her habitual tardiness, made by actor Peter Lawford on the night in 1962 when she sang her sizzling rendition of 'Happy Birthday' to President John Kennedy, and points out that . . .

'. . . the "late Marilyn Monroe" did not come late in life. It was not an affectation of stardom. She was late for her first *Life* cover . . .

'If you can imagine anyone as flamboyant as that being shy . . . I don't think there would have been a (*Life* magazine cover) if I hadn't been there to persuade the (*Life* photographer) to stick around (two extra hours); that she was worth it . . .'

Craft also saw the starstruck-fan side of Marilyn, and his insight illuminates another facet of her ambition:

'She would have liked to have done a Broadway play. Having grown up in Hollywood and been a part of that scene and so forth, she wasn't impressed by Hollywood. But she *was* enamoured of Broadway, and she wanted to be an actress, a *real* actress – I mean a Bette Davis-type actress.

'But it was a mistake, because she was such a consummate comedienne. She didn't realize it really. She could no more play in a Broadway play than I could pitch for the Yankees. She could never have made a curtain.'

However legendary, her tardiness wasn't

universal. She loved the singing and the dancing that she was called upon to do in her later movies, says Lionel Newman, at that time the head of the Fox music department and later to become senior vice president of music for features and television at the studio:

'She worked very hard and she loved the music portion of whatever she did. She was always on time for rehearsals, she was always on time to record; in fact, she was generally ahead of time. She'd be there when I was just reading something down, and I generally don't ask the artist to be there when I'm just checking for notes and so forth. But she was there. She was a remarkable girl.'

Like most others who knew her at the studio, Newman remarks on Marilyn's paradoxical mix of professionalism – even perfectionism – and insecurity. And that insecurity was, in turn, mixed with (and often mistaken for) vulnerability.

That Marilyn felt secure when she sang and danced is a point worth emphasizing. Many observers of her career point to the musical numbers as the highpoints of her art and the most delicious examples of her riveting screen presence.

As Newman himself points out, the singing-and-dancing abilities of Marilyn Monroe were a revelation to both the public and the studio's top executives . . . who at first actually found it hard to believe.

But by that time, Marilyn was at the height of her sex-goddess fame. And before she had the opportunity to display more than her spectacular physical charms, there would be several other pictures to do.

The Fireball/Early Stardom

Not only was 'The Fireball' the title of Marilyn's next film, it also is as apt a description as any of the next phase in her career. All of a sudden, it seemed, US movie screens exploded with picture after picture featuring Marilyn Monroe.

Between the end of 'All About Eve' in 1950 and 'Niagara' in 1953, Marilyn's first leading-woman dramatic role, came a succession of mostly less-than memorable pictures that fixed her sexy, dumb-blonde persona firmly in the public mind.

Her Fox movies in that period were:
'The Fireball' (1950)
'As Young As You Feel' (1951)
'Love Nest' (1951)
'Let's Make It Legal' (1951)
'We're Not Married' (1952)
'Don't Bother to Knock' (1952)
'Monkey Business' (1952)
'O. Henry's Full House' (1952)
In addition, Marilyn appeared in two pictures for MGM and one for RKO during these years.

Even if most of her parts were forgettable, she and the period were not. Although her trusted agent Johnny Hyde died shortly before this era began, on the whole these were 'the happy years' – as Roy Craft called them – of rising stardom and widening fame. These also were the years of increasing notoriety (when the public first learned of the nude calendar and the truth about her childhood) and of romance (Marilyn met both Joe DiMaggio and Arthur Miller during this period).

A number of thoughtful and informed observers have put forward differing explanations for the generally low quality of the films in which she played during this period. Was it a simple error in judgment by her then gravely ill agent to follow her stunning notices in 'Eve' with a non-speaking part in 'The Fireball', a Mickey Rooney vehicle set in the world of roller derby? Or was that part mandated by the terms and circumstances of her new seven-year contract with the studio? Perhaps it was simple coincidence.

Perhaps Marilyn herself was to blame – if 'blame' is the correct concept to apply to a question that touches on the imperatives of a collaborative art/business like Hollywood movie-making. Perhaps her dumb/sexy on-screen image gravitated naturally to what were then called 'B Pictures'. Perhaps the fault lies not in our star, but rather in the times during which she worked. The 1950s, after all, are generally regarded as a time of timidity in all the popular arts in America.

Then – as now – the great Hollywood corporations we know as 'studios' were subject to the same internecine feuds and executive wars that are the lot of all such complex institutions. Walter Scott's insight – what he is careful to characterize as 'purely my opinion' –

There was the same sort of electric response from the American public to Marilyn Monroe as there had been to child star, Shirley Temple, who at first was nothing but a cute little girl and then all of a sudden became a 'personality'.

takes cognizance of this fact of studio life. He observes that Marilyn's career was . . .

'. . . an uphill climb, because for some reason (production chief Darryl F.) Zanuck was not an enthusiastic booster of Marilyn Monroe.

'I always felt that it was probably because she was a protégée of (producer Joseph M.) Schenck . . .

'Although they were partners in Twentieth Century – Schenck being the money and Zanuck the production – there was a certain feeling that their social lives did not blend. In fact, you would never see Schenck and Zanuck at the same parties.'

Years earlier Schenck had been one of the forces behind the merger of Twentieth and Fox. Eventually, he became the earliest – and, arguably, the most powerful – of Marilyn's many patrons. Hollywood columnists of the period – as well as other, less suspect observers of Marilyn's career have asserted that she and Schenck – already a septuagenarian

when they first met – maintained a long-term love affair.

But as Lionel Newman observes, 'she wasn't a promiscuous girl'. He and a number of those who were closest to her are unanimous in describing the off-screen Marilyn as a person of simple, even plain, tastes. And as Newman and others point out, to claim to have had an affair with Marilyn Monroe was not only cheap, but easy, because it was difficult to refute.

Whatever the truth of their personal relationship, Marilyn's connection with Joe Schenck didn't prevent her from being saddled with small roles in second-rate pictures at a crucial juncture in her career.

In focusing on the huge publicity machine that geared up to propel Marilyn to stardom after her earliest successes, it is all too easy to ignore the crucial role of genuine public opinion. Unlike many of the other stars of the period that Fox – and its sister studios – nurtured and moulded, the phenomenon that was Marilyn Monroe forced the studio to

rush to keep up with a Marilyn-mad American public; hence, her co-starring billing in a number of films in which her part was no more than a walk-on (e.g. 'O. Henry's Full House') or a glorified cameo (e.g. 'As Young As You Feel').

Walter Scott makes a telling point about the Marilyn Monroe mania of that time. He notes that, in his career spanning five decades of film-making, he has seen only one other 'phenomenon' to compare to Marilyn. His comparison is as surprising as it is insightful:

'There was the same sort of electric response to Shirley Temple. At first, she was nothing but a cute little girl – a golden-haired child. Then all of a sudden, she was *something*; she was a personality . . .

'She lost it when she got older and, of course, Marilyn never had a chance to lose it.'

PICTURES OVERLEAF: Compare the plot synopsis for 'As Young As You Feel', which does not mention Marilyn at all, with the prominence given to her in the posters and promotional material.

SYNOPSIS
(Not for publication)

When John Hodges (MONTY WOOLLEY), a hand-press operator gets fired from the Acme Printing Company because he has reached the retirement age of 65, the home of George (ALLYN JOSLYN) and Della Hodges (THELMA RITTER) really becomes upset. Alice Hodges' (JEAN PETERS) romance with Joe Elliott (DAVID WAYNE) teeters on the brink of disaster and the economic welfare of the household reaches a new low.

John has no intention of staying fired, however, and when he learns that the retirement policy of Acme is dictated by its parent company, Consolidated Motors, he gets an idea. Posing as the president of Consolidated Motors, John sends a letter to Acme's president Louis McKinley (ALBERT DEKKER) advising him that he will be visiting the plant on an inspection tour. The red carpet is laid out for him.

John arrives in the guise of Cleveland and immediately starts his campaign to have all the old men of the company retained in their jobs. Then he is catapulted into a situation he had not bargained for. He is asked to speak at the Chamber of Commerce luncheon and his remarks go out over the radio and get prominent space in the newspapers. They cover the Capital and Labor situation in such a sound manner that the officers of Consolidated Motors and particularly President Cleveland are thrown into confusion. Since the stock market reacts favorably and Consolidated Motors goes up, they cannot repudiate the speech.

Another complication develops at the country club when John is entertained by Mr. and Mrs. McKinley (CONSTANCE BENNETT). She is so impressed with the attention John shows her, she thinks she has fallen in love with him.

The McKinley household is upset too, with Mrs. McKinley declaring that she intends getting a divorce. At the Acme office, Joe's rival divulges John's identity and McKinley prepares reprisals against his wife and John. When McKinley arrives at the Hodges' home looking for his wife, who has come to tell John that she loves him, he sees John and fires him. John persuades Lucille to go back to her husband. Della sees the money for highpriced soup bones coming in again when Cleveland firmly entrenches John in his old job and a most amusing set of circumstances are straightened out happily for all.

Years later, Marilyn herself attributed her sudden stardom to another source: just as the GIs of an earlier generation had made Betty Grable a star by carrying her pin-ups to war, so did the soldiers in Korea make Marilyn a star in the early 1950s. Once pin-ups of her had been distributed overseas, her fanmail from the troops increased tenfold – Marilyn reported – convincing the studio heads of her potential with the public.

Marilyn's next Fox film was 'As Young As You Feel'. Playwright Paddy Chayefsky's original story-for-the-screen was entitled 'The Great American Hoax' and told a fanciful fable about a sixty-five-year-old worker (Monty Woolley) at a small printing company, who, after mandatory retirement, dyes his hair and impersonates the real-life figure of Charles Wilson, then head of real-life automotive conglomerate General Motors. (Wilson, of 'What's good for General Motors is good for the country' fame, became US Secretary of Defence during the Eisenhower administration.) In Chayefsky's story

General Motors was the corporate owner of the small printing company.

This witty and pungent tale became 'a picture about a wonderful family – for the whole family to see': in it, the retired worker, now impersonating the president of fictitious *Consolidated* Motors, returns to inspect the printing company – where Marilyn Monroe is the secretary to the small firm's president.

Monroe's role was small and strictly decorative, and in most cast credit sheets she received sixth billing (after Woolley, who had been a popular and critical success in 'The Man Who Came to Dinner', Thelma Ritter, David Wayne and Jean Peters). Yet it was Marilyn who was featured most prominently in the picture's posters and advertising.

Exhibitor's Campaign Books were a compendium of poster art and puffery that Fox (and other studios) sent to theatre owners and potential film bookers. Compare the posters reprinted from the original 'Young' Campaign Book to the plot synopsis from that same book which does not mention Marilyn at all.

A publicity article from the same Exhibitor's Campaign Book alludes – in typical press-agent language of the period – to the tension that was developing between the dumb-blonde cheesecake image, already formed in the public's imagination, and Marilyn's dramatic ambitions: '*MARILYN WANTS A CHANCE TO SHOW WHAT SHE'S GOT*', the headline leers. And the story's first sentence explains that, '*Contrary to reports, starlet Marilyn Monroe will not renounce cheesecake art for a dramatic career, but will try for a happy medium of the two.*'

The picture – the anonymous publicity writer explains – offers Marilyn 'ample chance to display both her charms as well as her histrionic prowess.'

The article also 'quotes' a very un-Marilyn-sounding Marilyn Monroe:

'In announcing her decision to keep a middle acting course, Marilyn declared: "After all, there is nothing wrong, that I can see, in having a sound, healthy body. If anything, I think that cheesecake art has given my career a big boost. I believe that it has helped me to get ahead more quickly than if I had not done any." But, realizing that mere physical beauty is not enough in the long run, Marilyn is quick to add that: "At Twentieth Century Fox they haven't overlooked a single opportunity to give me roles in which I have been called on to engage in dramatics. For that I am eternally grateful."'

Two pages later, under a picture of Marilyn and the headline '*Quite A Gal!*' the Campaign Book informs potential exhibitors that . . .

'. . . the honey-tressed actress with the most provocative chassis to reach the screen since Jean Harlow, has five wardrobe changes – each a sweater of a different type – in "As Young As You Feel".'

Continued on page 51

MAT—220

52 Lines x 2 Cols. (104 Lines)
(2 Cols. x 3¾ Inches)

MAT—221

52 Lines x 2 Cols. (104 Lines)
(2 Cols. x 3¾ Inches)

Marilyn Monroe, the azure-eyed, honey-tressed actress with the most provocative chassis to reach the screen since Jean Harlow, has five wardrobe changes — each a sweater of a different type—in "As Young As You Feel," Twentieth Century-Fox's new comedy coming next to the .... Theatre.

Cast as a siren in the Twentieth Century-Fox comedy which stars Monty Woolley, Thelma Ritter, David Wayne and Jean Peters, Marilyn's sweaters are described by the costuming department as:

1. Loose fitting.
2. Draping.
3. Clinging.
4. Tight.
5. Gee-whizz!!!   (Mat 1A)

Albert Dekker finds it hard to keep his mind on business when luscious Marilyn Monroe is the secretary in question in Twentieth Century-Fox's new comedy "As Young As You Feel," now playing at the .... Theatre. The film co-stars Monty Woolley, Thelma Ritter, David Wayne and Jean Peters.   Mat 2D, Still No. 816/13

Page Four

THIS PAGE AND OPPOSITE: Marilyn in the role of
secretary with Albert Dekter in 'As Young As
You Feel'.

Copyright © Twentieth Century Fox Film Corporation

She had just begun her long-term contract, but already it was obvious that the starlet with the small part in 'Young' had a big part to play in the picture's potential success.

Next from Fox was 'Love Nest' (originally titled 'A Wac in His Life'), in which Marilyn is the 'old army buddy' whose arrival at a New York boarding house almost disrupts an ex-GI's marriage.

Once again, the part was small, but the publicity build-up for Marilyn was huge.

Even before the picture was released, the American public was being treated to the publicity-machine version of the full-blown Monroe Legend, in which Truth, Beauty and Hype coexisted in perfect, albeit mirage-like balance. A *Colliers* article of the period, by Robert Cahn, describes Marilyn's arrival in a 'strapless black cocktail gown' at a Fox commissary gathering for 'bigwigs and freshly manicured salesmen', at which stars like Susan Hayward, Anne Baxter, Gregory Peck and Tyrone Power mingled:

'Already a studio vice-president and two producers, suddenly self-designated Prince Charmings, had converged on the late arrival. A moment later, she was wafted off to the upper echelons, her progress punctuated by the popping of flash bulbs as visitors pressed forward to have their pictures taken with her. Finally, as the guests sat down for dinner, the blonde was installed at the head of the No. 1 table, at the right hand of company president Spyros Skouras.

'While the long-established female stars silently measured her, young Marilyn Monroe, who has engaged less than 50 minutes' screen time, stole the show.'

Cahn calls the Fox press offensive for Marilyn the 'biggest publicity build-up since the Jane Russell campaign'.

Nonetheless, she is 'a disturbing presence', who 'caused a small crisis when she appeared in a red and white polka-dot Bikini' on the set of 'Love Nest'.

The article concludes with an almost point-by-point recitation of the major elements of the Marilyn myth:

She spends 'hours at the make-up table in preparation for even commonplace engagements . . . if each day had 30 hours, Marilyn would use them all in getting ready.'

She has 'a childhood eagerness to please . . . Marilyn is still a shy, uncertain girl, who takes solitary pleasure in long early-morning walks up and down the vacant Beverly Hills alleys, clad in old shirts and faded blue jeans. She has an oppressive awareness of the swift passage of time and her own perishability . . .'

She 'lives in a small Beverly Hills apartment, with few of the fairy princess trappings that she once dreamed about and can now afford . . .'

She has 'an insatiable desire . . . to learn new things. At night school (in a UCLA literature course) she is constantly pestering the student next to her to find out what certain big words mean.'

And, of course, she is 'impatient to prove herself in something more than supporting parts'.

The *Colliers* writer concludes with a quote – from Marilyn herself – about her *other* ambition: 'Someday I want to have a house of my own with trees and grass and hedges all around, but never trim them at all – just let them grow any old way they want.'

That concluding quotation is an example of another important aspect of the Marilyn mystique; namely, an exceptional body of remarks – sometimes allusive, sometimes suggestive, often hilariously funny – which are commonly thought to have been written for her by the army of press agents masterminded by Fox 'publicity genius' Harry Brand.

But Roy Craft, the man most often thought to have written her most famous comments, denies it; Marilyn was the spontaneous author of her own quips, he maintains.

And former publicist Johnny Campbell agrees that Marilyn 'understood what the public wanted better than Harry Brand, one of the great gods of Hollywood publicity'.

Be that as it may, a pre-title change press release on 'A Wac in His Life', sent out by Brand, contains an interesting passage about Marilyn – especially in light of a similar but, as it were, opposite anecdote related by Whitey Snyder and others. The Brand press release notes rather breathlessly that:

'Marilyn, who claims that walking is the perfect exercise to retain the curves of her classical chassis, tried walking to and from the studio at the start of the picture. She abandoned the project after the first day when gallant male motorists persisted in stopping to offer her lifts.'

Whitey and a number of others who knew her best point out that Marilyn the Sex Goddess was an on-screen, in-public fantasy figure, who was not present in Marilyn's personal life. In private, at home or with her few close friends, Marilyn wore neither make-up nor Hollywood finery. Whitey remembers that . . .

'She used to play down at my boat in the Marina. Put a bandanna around her head and nobody would know who she was . . . She'd go down to Ocean Park (at that time, an amusement park) and play around (on the rides) and come home, and nobody would know the difference.'

Contrary to Brand's traffic-stopping siren, Whitey's comparable story has a different twist:

One morning – he recalls – Marilyn, then residing near Beverly Hills, a few miles from the studio, found herself without a car. Either she had lent it to her drama coach, Natasha Lytess, and it hadn't yet been returned, or Natasha or

Continued on page 55

Teeth bared, Marilyn Monroe enacts an ex-WAC buddy of William Lundigan's who intrudes on his subsequent marriage to June Haver in "Love Nest," romantic comedy-with-complications now at the .... Theatre. Frank Fay is also starred in the Twentieth Century-Fox hit.

Mat 1A.   Still No. 825/36

TRAILER TREATMENT

The Trailer for "Love Nest" is bright and breezy in the same manner as the film itself. Young, pert entertainment, its motif is carried out in the Trailer. Order it from National Screen Service:

TITLES:

(Over clinch Lundigan & Haver)
LOVE YOUTH? . . .
LOVE EXCITEMENT? . .
LOVE ROLLICKING FUN? . . .
(Haver, Lundigan, Monroe drink toast)
(Shot of Haver and Lundigan in bedroom . . . winding up with clinch)
Then MOST CERTAINLY YOU'LL LOVE . . .
"LOVE NEST"
(Shot of Lundigan and Haver climbing stairs)
FOR EVERYONE WHO EVER BUILT
A STAIRWAY TO THE STARS . . .
(Clinch on stairs)
AND CLIMBED IT KISS BY KISS!

NARRATOR:

(Monroe undresses—freeze frame and hold)
(Lundigan asleep on sofa in foreground)
Now wait a minute . . . hold everything . . .
what's coming off here. . .
(reverse film for effect on putting clothes back on)
get back into those thing, young lady . . .
while we take a better look at the intimates of this hilarious house . . .

TITLES:

WILLIAM LUNDIGAN—This is Jim, who has his hands full
with a blonde in his arms in the basement . . .
(Monroe smiles at Lundigan as he sleeps on sofa)
and a cutie on his mind upstairs . . .
JUNE HAVER
(Haver dresses to go out shopping)
here's Connie . . . a landlord who makes paying your rent a pleasure . . .
FRANK FAY
(Fay kissing hand and in intimate discussion with 3 different women)
that's Charlie . . . he has more love affairs than he can get away with.
MARILYN MONROE
(Monroe in bathing suit reclining in yard)
and this is Bobbie . . . and old army buddy who just got
back to her base of operations . . . Wow!
(Scenes)

NARRATOR:

The police arrive in the nick of time . . .
The plumbing goes out most of the time . . .
And the walls rock with fun and laughter all the time . . .
in the screen's most heart-warming house-warming in years!

TITLES:

JUNE HAVER — WILLIAM LUNDIGAN
    FRANK FAY — MARILYN MONROE
        JACK PAAR in
        "LOVE NEST"
Produced by   Directed by
JULES BUCK   Joseph Newman
        A 20th Century-Fox Picture
C'MON A OUR HOUSE . . .
WE'LL GIVE YOU LOVIN'
AND LAUGHIN' AND EVERYTHING!

EXHIBITOR'S CAMPAIGN BOOK

MAT—300

166 lines x 3 cols. (498 lines)
(3 cols. x 11⅞ inches)

Extra Publicity Gimmick

Incorporated into the campaign is an extra publicity gimmick in the form of a coupon at bottom of ad, which can be clipped out and mailed in for a free pin-up picture of Marilyn Monroe. This attractive "extra" insures added Marilyn Monroe consciousness and 'Love Nest" box-office.

another studio official simply had failed to arrive at Marilyn's apartment to drive her to work. Although he doesn't recall what *exactly* prompted her to start off on her own, Whitey is certain of what happened next . . . Marilyn decided to hitch a ride, but . . .

'Nobody picked her up . . . Monroe was hitch-hiking to the studio from her apartment near Beverly Hills, and she hitch-hiked down Santa Monica boulevard and *nobody would pick her up.*

'When she finally got to the studio, she said, "Gee, I had to walk all the way."'

'Let's Make It Legal', Marilyn's next Fox picture, followed the by-then familiar pattern: a bit part as a dumb/shrewd blonde, with critical notices that mostly reviewed her 'shapely chassis'.

Marilyn co-starred in this light marital farce along with Claudette Colbert, Macdonald Carey and Zachary Scott. But in a one-hundred-and-thirteen-page script, she had a scant fourteen lines.

The script introduces her as . . . 'A very pretty girl in a pretty bathing suit, (who) comes by the pool and waves warmly . . . she is young, womanly, and blonde.'

'We're Not Married', an 'all-star comedy of marital confusion', followed.

Marilyn had fourth billing and a part (as an aspiring beauty queen) that was as substantial as any in this episodic Nunnally Johnson script.

The Exhibitor's Campaign Book for 'Married' teams Marilyn with Zsa Zsa Gabor, describing them as America's 'dream girls' and 'high-riding favourite beauties of the day'.

Exhibitors also were offered 'an array of Marilyn Monroe specially posed art that is surefire material for lavish local newspaper planting.' In those days, as in these, battalions of press agents were in the employ of all the major studios; 'planting' (that is arranging in one fashion or another to have published) articles and photos in the newspapers of the cities in which a film was playing was always of major concern.

Then, as now, motion picture merchandising 'tie-ins' were important to distributors and exhibitors alike. Once again, Marilyn was an important draw.

Marilyn's next Fox picture was a departure. 'Don't Bother to Knock' was her first major dramatic role. In it, she played a mentally disturbed babysitter, who attracts the attentions of a flyer (Richard Widmark). The *noire*-style film had an overwrought script and was a box-office failure. Marilyn's critical notices were mixed, however, with more

than one critic remarking on her 'promise' as an actress.

Marilyn's next two pictures returned her to the successful formula. In 'O. Henry's Full House', an anthology film based on several O. Henry short stories, she had a 'walk-on' part as a streetwalker, playing opposite Charles Laughton, in the 'Cop and the Anthem' episode of the film.

As befits a motion picture constructed from the short stories of an author who is a secondary-school literature-class staple, the Exhibitor's Book for 'Full House' suggested tie-ins with schools, booksellers and 'influential people in all walks of life'.

Nonetheless, the Exhibitor's Book urges Marilyn fans to be 'reassured' that . . .

'Marilyn Monroe shows her shape in "O. Henry's Full House", the all-star, five-part movie now at the . . . . Theatre, only through two bustles. This is Miss Monroe's first involvement with period costume, and those who have seen the picture report she meets the challenge nobly.

'Naturally, Miss Monroe is more at home in a bathing suit, wherein she was last on view in "We're Not Married", another multiple movie in the current popularity of "episode" pictures.'

OPPOSITE (LEFT TO RIGHT): Macdonald Carey, Marilyn Monroe and Barbara Bates in 'Let's Make It Legal', a light marital farce in which Marilyn co-starred along with Claudette Colbert, Macdonald Carey and Zachary Scott.

THIS PAGE: A few quick adjustments between takes!

Both copyright © Twentieth Century Fox Film Corporation

*BATHING *BEAUTY *CONTEST

Enter into the summertime spirit of your "We're Not Married" release by staging a Bathing Beauty Contest in co-operation with local beaches or municipal pools. Preliminaries to be conducted by swim instructors and life guards, semi-finals and finals at the theatre prior to and during engagement. Approach to the girls should be along these lines: "Do You Look Like Marilyn Monroe? Enter the WE'RE NOT MARRIED Bathing Beauty Contest." Appropriate prizes can be promoted from local dealers, with passes to playdate for runner-up entrants. Presentation of cup to winner can be made on stage of theatre.

ABOVE AND OPPOSITE PAGE: Material from the Exhibitor's Campaign Book for 'We're Not Married'. This teamed Marilyn with Zsa-Zsa Gabor, describing them as America's 'dream girls' and 'high-riding favourite beauties of the day'. Exhibitors were also offered merchandising tie-ins and an array of Marilyn Monroe specially posed poster art.

All copyright © Twentieth Century Fox Film Corporation

Bountiful Blondes

Marilyn Monroe (left) and Zsa Zsa Gabor, two of Hollywood's most sizzling blonde personalities, put their talents to ample use in Twentieth Century-Fox's all-star comedy, "We're Not Married," the next attraction at the .... Theatre.

Mat 2W

SPECIAL MARILYN MONROE ART FOR LOCAL NEWSPAPER BREAKS

Girl Friend

Hottest New Star Is 'Talk of Hollywood'

Here's an array of Marilyn Monroe specially-posed art that is surefire material for lavish local newspaper planting. Editors everywhere have labeled her the "hottest new personality since Jean Harlow." She's truly "the talk of Hollywood"—and the world. And a natural to make the papers for your "We're Not Married" playdate.

By the Beautiful Sea

Sitting on Top of the World

Above (Left to Right): (1) Mat SP 1A; (2) Mat SP 4A; (3) Mat SP 2A

Order All Mats from National Screen Service
Be Sure That Newspaper Captions Credit Your "We're Not Married" Playdate

AMERICA'S LEADING MAGAZINES SALUTE "WE'RE NOT MARRIED" DREAM GIRLS!

They're Both In "We're Not Married" Exploit Them To The Hilt!

Marilyn Monroe On Cover of LIFE!

Zsa Zsa Gabor On Cover of LOOK!

It's not often you get a picture starring *both* of the high-riding favorite beauties of the day, but you have exactly that in "We're Not Married." The girls winning top space and the most coveted magazine breaks in America today are Marilyn Monroe, shown here on a recent cover of LIFE, and Zsa Zsa Gabor, highlighting a recent cover of LOOK. This is publicity penetration of the most effective kind—everyone sees the covers of these top magazines. And it's a direct build-up for your "We're Not Married" playdate. Cash in with a prominent lobby display piece reproducing these issues in large blow-ups with appropriate copy added.

'Don't Bother To Knock' was Marilyn's first major dramatic role. In it, she played a mentally disturbed baby-sitter, who attracts the attentions of a flyer (Richard Widmark). The *noire*-style film had an overwrought script and was a box-office failure. Marilyn's notices were mixed, however, with more than one critic remarking on her 'promise' as an actress.

ABOVE: 'One-sheet' of 'Don't Bother To Knock', in which Marilyn is described as being 'a wicked sensation as the lonely girl in Room 809'.

OPPOSITE PAGE: Publicity still from the film.
Both pictures copyright © Twentieth Century Fox Film Corporation

850·R·1

ABOVE AND OPPOSITE: Two stills from 'O. Henry's Full House', a five-part anthology film based on several O. Henry short stories. Marilyn had a 'walk-on' part as a street-walker, playing opposite Charles Laughton in the 'Cop and the Anthem' episode of the film. The Exhibitor's Campaign Book for the film notes 'This is Miss Monroe's first involvement with period costume, and those who have seen the picture report she meets the challenge nobly.'
Both photographs copyright © Twentieth Century Fox Film Corporation

A Niagara Of Monkey Business

'Monkey Business', a feathery-light comedy in which she co-starred with Cary Grant and Ginger Rogers, featured Marilyn in yet another sexy-secretary role.

Perhaps the most famous lines in the Howard Hawks-directed farce about a pixilated professor (Grant), who accidentally discovers a youth serum, were in the repartee between Grant and Rogers (playing husband and wife) about the character played by Marilyn:

'She's just a half-infant,' says Grant dismissively.

'Not the half that's visible,' Rogers snaps in return.

That 'visible-half' remark may have resonated with suggestive meaning for film audiences of the time, who only then were learning the truth about Marilyn's background and, especially, about her nude calendar.

The entire calendar-revelation episode shows a Marilyn Monroe who was either very lucky or very shrewd when it came to her own publicity – shrewder than the best press agents in Hollywood.

'She had the most incredible PR luck,' recalls Johnny Campbell, pointing to the Miss America Grand Marshal photo that a misguided military officer tried to kill . . . thereby ensuring that the very next day every newspaper editor in the country ran the photo of Marilyn and a group of servicewomen in uniform.

Roy Craft, the former Fox publicist

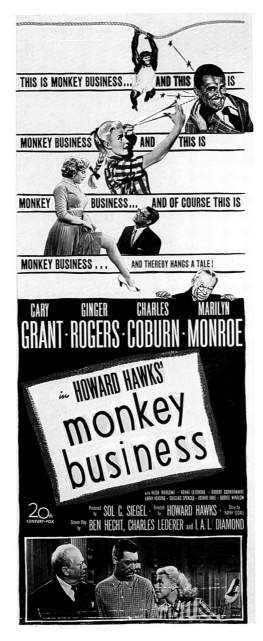

who specialized in 'pretty girl' pictures, remembers that incident vividly. In conjunction with the première of 'Monkey Business' in New York, Marilyn had been named Grand Marshal of the 1952 Miss America pageant in nearby Atlantic City, NJ – a high honour usually reserved for the likes of dignified politicos or hero-soldiers.

But that year, thanks to a 'convincing' Fox publicist on the East Coast, the famed beauty pageant got more than it bargained for. Marilyn Monroe was named Grand Marshal, and 'she just murdered those poor little Miss Americas'. All attention was on her, and one of her first duties was greeting the various state winners as they arrived . . .

'And Miss California would come in, and there would be a picture service back to California papers. And Miss Oregon or Miss Colorado or whatever . . .

'And this was like canning tomatoes, all day long it would go on. So during the day a young major came in from the Pentagon with four service girls in uniform . . . the real Miss Americas are the girls who are serving their country, the WAC and the WAVE and the lady Coast Guard and so on.

'So they lined up for a picture – just a family-album type shot, with Marilyn in the middle and these four girls in their uniforms.

'It was a routine shot, but the UP guy had gotten up on a chair and shot down.

Continued on page 68

Marilyn played yet another sexy secretary role in 'Monkey Business'. THIS PAGE AND OPPOSITE: Publicity material from the Exhibitor's Campaign Book for the film.
All pictures copyright © Twentieth Century Fox Film Corporation

Cary Grant, wearing glasses for emphasis, is getting some solid instruction in the term "leg art" from one who should know—Marilyn Monroe—in this enticing view of "Monkey Business," gay Twentieth Century-Fox comedy opening .... at the .... Theatre. For good measure, Ginger Rogers and Charles Coburn also star in the merry romp.
Still No. 856/15, Mat 2D

e frisk is on the froth in the new movie frolic, "Monkey Business," v at the .... Theatre. In the example shown here, Cary Grant down for the count, but who wouldn't tumble for Marilyn Monroe?
Still No. 856/75, Mat 2F

In the swim, and plainly loving it, are Cary Grant and Marilyn Monroe, stars of "Monkey Business," the Twentieth Century-Fox howl regaling audiences at the .... Theatre for a .... week. Ginger Rogers and Charles Coburn are also starred in the sparkler, which was pro-duced by Sol C. Siegel and directed by Howard Hawks.
Still No. 856/76, Mat 2C

OPPOSITE PAGE (TOP THREE PHOTOGRAPHS): Marilyn, Cary Grant and director Howard Hawks during the filming of 'Monkey Business'.

THIS PAGE AND OPPOSITE (BELOW): 'Monkey Business' publicity stills.

The result was quite a bit of what we called "cleavage" in those innocent days. To look at it now, it was nothing.

'This was serviced (to papers) around the country. A lot better art came out of Atlantic City, so this picture went out and (was) just stuck aside.

'Then along about nine or ten o'clock at night, the young major came in to press headquarters and thumbed through the pictures. He saw this picture of the service girls with a bosomy Marilyn. And he had been told when he left Washington to not have his girls do any cheesecake art – they meant not have the (service) girls show their legs or any of that, to be on their good behaviour. But he saw this (picture) and ordered it killed.

'So UPI bulletined across the country that the army had ordered this picture with Monroe killed. Naturally, the editors across the country dived down onto the pile and broke (the picture) out. Hell, in LA it was the whole top of the front page . . .'

The episode resulted in one of the few times that Craft made up a Marilyn quip. She was already in bed that night by the time UPI called, wanting a reaction to the attempted suppression of the photo . . .

'I said Marilyn had retired, but I'd get a statement from her and call them back.

'So I hung up and waited a decent interval – I wasn't going to get her out of bed at that time of night – and called back and said that Marilyn said that she had meant nothing but to honour the service girls.

'She'd noticed that people had been looking at her all day, but she thought they'd been looking at her Grand Marshal's badge.

'So that gave them a quote and that was all they needed.'

The press wanted anything it could get about Marilyn – partly to feed the public's insatiable curiosity, of course, and partly because Marilyn herself was

such good copy. And in those years, Marilyn's own instincts about the press and publicity seemed infallible.

The nude-calendar revelation was perhaps the most outstanding case in point. She offered the news to a reporter herself, against almost all advice. As Johnny Campbell remembers it:

'(Reporter) Ilene Mosby broke the story. Marilyn said (during an interview), "Please follow me up to the restroom," where she confessed all, against the advice everybody gave.

'She didn't want to confess in front of . . . the unit publicist who was at the interview. And as to *why* she wanted to confess, I think she did it because she understood the American public better than Harry Brand (Fox PR Director), who was one of the great figures of Hollywood publicity.

'She'd been warned not to do it. (Tom) Kelley, the (calendar) photographer, . . . wouldn't admit that it was Marilyn. And they (the publicity officials) thought that it would destroy a career of great promise . . .

'It turned out to be one of the great publicity coups. And I think she understood all that instinctively.'

By the time of 'Monkey Business' even the refinements in her blonde hair colour from picture to picture were a subject of press interest – this despite the fact that many of her films were in black-and-white. Accordingly, the Exhibitor's Book for 'Monkey Business' featured an article on the picture-by-picture colour variations in the 'atomic blonde''s coif.

And once again, the Exhibitor's Book came with a suggestion for a Marilyn

EXPLOITATION EXTRAS!

Secretary Contest

Marilyn Monroe is Cary Grant's blonde secretary in "Monkey Business." Run a contest for secretaries on your theatre stage to determine the local secretary closest to Marilyn's qualifications: height 5' 5½", weight 118, hair blonde, eyes blue, bust 36, waist 25. Side-by-side photos of Miss Monroe and the winner good for a photo break in the local papers; interview with the winner's local boss a surefire newspaper feature.

Laughing Record

To emphasize the laughing-room-only aspect of your "Monkey Business" playdate, keep your theatre front lively with a continuous playing laugh record hooked up to your house front public address system.

As The Blondes Go, Marilyn's Chameleon

"Some girls prefer to change hats. I just prefer to change my hair color," says Marilyn Monroe, starred with Cary Grant, Ginger Rogers and Charles Coburn in Twentieth Century-Fox's "Monkey Business," now at the . . . . Theatre.

Most gentlemen who prefer blondes prefer Marilyn Monroe, and probably never notice from one picture to the next that the exact color of her blondeness is never the same twice. Nor do they seem to care if they do notice.

When one writer carpingly referred to Marilyn as the "chameleon blonde," Marilyn felt it necessary to come to her own defense. "The changes give me a lift, and certainly we owe it to the fans to give them a change," she states. "We can't very well switch faces, but actresses can and should avoid monotony by changing the personality of their coiffeures and clothes. It gives me a transformed feeling."

Marilyn started out an ash blonde in "The Asphalt Jungle," switched to golden blonde for her showgirl role in "All About Eve," was silver blonde in "As Young As You Feel," amber blonde in "Let's Make It Legal," and smokey blonde in "Love Nest."

They called it alabaster blonde in "Clash By Night," topaz blonde in "We're Not Married" and honey blonde in "O. Henry's Full House." They didn't know what to call it in "Don't Bother to Knock," because for her first serious dramatic role of consequence Marilyn refused to change her natural color, a dark, golden brown.

In "Monkey Business" it's

And now a lady who needs no introduction, Miss Marilyn Monroe, the favorite pin-up girl of just about everybody. At the moment you can see her in "Monkey Business" at the .... Theatre, along with Cary Grant, Ginger Rogers and Charles Coburn.

Mat 1B

been dubbed champagne blonde, after the phrase "butter blonde" was turned down as too yellow. "But I prefer beer," Marilyn points out. "It's really a prettier color than champagne, but I suppose it doesn't sound as glamorous." Most will agree that by any other name Marilyn Monroe is still the atomic blonde first.

Monroe lookalike contest for the 'local secretary closest to Marilyn's qualifications: height 5'5½", weight 118, hair blonde, eyes blue, bust 36, waist 25.'

The hoopla surrounding the Miss America episode provides a number of examples of Marilyn's own sure publicity acumen – as well as of her tardiness that was by then spreading like a kind of molasses to impede the smooth functioning of the studio publicity machine.

Roy Craft and others involved in her scheduling during that period recall that the tardiness became such a problem that if she had an appointment at four in the afternoon, for example, they would tell her it was scheduled for two; nonetheless, she would invariably be late.

The sensation Marilyn caused at the Miss America pageant almost didn't happen for that reason, Roy Craft recalls:

'We were in New York, en route to Atlantic City for this grand opening (parade) . . .

'Marilyn had wanted to take to New York her own hairdresser, but the studio thought that was unnecessary and supplied her with a New York hairdresser. Whether that had anything to do with (what happened), I don't know. But anyway, we missed the train.

'Everything was on a precision schedule, and we were supposed to take a certain train from New York to Atlantic City. And there was a high-school band there at the (Atlantic City) station to meet her and the Mayor and Miss America officials and so forth.

'Well, we get down to the dad-gummed railroad station and the train had pulled out. We were late again.

'A young publicity man was with us and he got a hold of the New York office (of the studio) and, to make the story short, they chartered an airplane.

'Now, the only thing they could charter on quick notice was a forty-five place passenger plane. We dashed out to the airfield . . . get on this plane and head for Atlantic City.

'The only people aboard were the crew – the pilot and copilot and a male steward that they'd rushed into service – and the other press agent and Marilyn and me.

'Now, we get aboard the plane and Marilyn quietly takes a nap, oblivious to everything. We landed at the Atlantic (City) airport, which is about ten miles out of town, as I recall. They had sheriffs there with cars, and we went a-screaming through the countryside, with chickens flying out of the way and everything – a real dramatic deal.

'And we get into the Atlantic City railroad station just as the train got there. So Marilyn boarded the train, then made her exit as though nothing had happened.'

What probably happened next that day is recalled by Johnny Campbell as another ironic example of Marilyn's publicity 'luck':

'On some parade – I think on the same (Atlantic City) adventure – she was late and really caused a lot of trouble.

'She was always late, (but) sometimes it caused trouble and sometimes it didn't. This time it did and Roy really raised hell with her.

'And it ended up with the chairman of the parade giving poor Roy hell for treating this nice young woman so badly.'

But, as usual, once Marilyn finally got in front of the public everything went splendidly. Craft recalls the Miss America boardwalk parade, headed by Grand Marshal Marilyn Monroe:

'Marilyn was in a car and she was leading the parade.

'All the press was going right ahead of Marilyn, taking pictures, right down the boardwalk. The poor little Miss Americas, they were just terribly neglected.

'Marilyn had a bunch of flowers in the (car). And the people would riot – I mean, they'd rush up and there would be this awful time clearing them out of the way. And they'd proceed a little way down the boardwalk.

'The minute things would slow down a little, Marilyn would throw another rose. And then, here they'd come again . . .'

That magical, ultra-glamorous in-person aura was not something to which only the unsophisticated public responded. Examples abound of how Hollywood's biggest stars themselves weren't immune.

Oscar-winner Walter Scott remembers a Hollywood awards night during this period:

'It was *Photoplay* or one of those other annual magazine awards that they always held in the Crystal Room of the Beverly Hills Hotel.

'This particular award they were going to have several big stars attend, and they kept delaying and delaying because Marilyn wasn't there. And it was really quite late.

'The Crystal Room has a marvellous entrance stairway. You come in on an upper level and you (then) come down a stairway.

'Everyone kept saying, "She's not going to show, she's not going to show." And all of a sudden, whatever they were doing behind the microphone to carry on the ceremonies of the evening just stopped.

'And out of nowhere, Marilyn in white satin appears at the top of the stairs.

'She just stood there a moment, having absolutely stunned the audience. Then about six of the biggest stars in Hollywood went dashing over to the stairway to assist her down into the room.

'It was a moment – God! – you don't forget: this girl just absolutely *stunned* that room, and by just standing at the top of the stairs . . .

'I tell you it was just magic, complete magic, the effect she had on that whole audience. Here you have the biggest stars in Hollywood all over the place, at every table . . . In those days, in the early '50s, it was almost a command performance when the movie magazines gave awards; everyone who was anyone was invited. And she was just emerging, you might say, just becoming a real star. But the point is, *everyone* was waiting for this particular person to appear.'

Marilyn Monroe now was the centre of attention wherever she went. She was the centre of a great deal of notoriety, too. A number of versions exist of one of the most prominent of those controversies; that is, the censorious public umbrage taken by Joan Crawford over a supposedly 'scandalous' dress that Marilyn wore to an awards ceremony.

Roy Craft and others recall a *Photoplay* awards dinner and a revealing velvet dress, designed by Bill Travilla, the great Hollywood designer responsible for most of Marilyn's most stunning movie costumes. Others say the dress was the form-fitting gold lamé gown she wore in 'Gentlemen Prefer Blondes'.

Marilyn herself, in the fragmentary autobiography that was published posthumously by her one-time business partner, Milton Greene (Stein and Day, 1974), remembers that it was an Academy Awards ceremony. According to Marilyn, Joan Crawford told the newspapers that her behaviour at the Awards evening had been tasteless and undignified. She was apparently criticised by Crawford for appearing in a figure-hugging dress, which left little to the imagination especially when viewed from the rear, as she walked by with the characteristic Marilyn hip-sway holding an Oscar award.

ABOVE: Marilyn and Roy Craft at an awards
dinner. Says Craft: 'She wasn't being awarded
anything, as I recall, but stole the show. I don't
know who or what I appear to be warding off,
certainly not the press.'
Copyright © Twentieth Century Fox Film Corporation

Marilyn goes on to report a comment on the affair by an unnamed friend, who advised her to forgive the lady who had herself been young and sexy once.

That passing remark, easily dismissed simply as 'catty', would have been portentous to those in the know in the early 1950s. A page later in the autobiography, Marilyn tells of a writer who assuages her fears about the negative publicity attending the nude calendar revelation by assuring her that a girl on the brink of movie stardom in the twenties had experienced the same thing when she became famous after Hollywood producers discovered that she had appeared entirely naked in a stag film.

The public knows now what the public of the time never suspected: Crawford was neither the model mother *nor* the figure of moral perfection depicted by *her* publicity machine, and it was she who had performed in the early silent stag film.

Marilyn ends the anecdote by having the 'writer' report that the girl became famous a few months after these revelations and remained in the public eye thereafter, to which Marilyn added the remark that she was also one of her biggest critics.

Nonetheless, the entire episode became grist (or rather, in this case, tubers) for the publicity mill. When, in the wake of the contretemps, a newspaper columnist remarked that Marilyn would look good even in a potato sack, Craft and his cohorts cooked up a publicity photo of Marilyn in just such a sack. Says Craft:

'I picked up an Idaho potato sack from a produce dealer and designer Billy Travilla draped it on Marilyn after fringing the bottom. With us that day was Travilla, Whitey the make-up man, a body make-up woman, hairdresser, wardrobe mistress, plus cameraman, etc. The result was this simple snapshot that went all over the world and the Idaho potato association was nice enough to ship a

couple of sacks of No. 1 spuds to Marilyn.'

And of course, she *did* look good even in a potato sack.

During this period, Marilyn met both of her husbands-to-be. Arthur Miller made an appearance on one set and, later, Joe DiMaggio, whom Marilyn had just started to date, turned up on another. (Craft and other publicists report scheming to get a picture of Marilyn and DiMaggio, who was reluctant to be photographed, during the filming of

'Monkey Business'. The great Yankee baseball player relented when a shot including Cary Grant was proposed. After the threesome was duly photographed, the wily publicists snipped Grant out of the shot, which was then sent out to newspapers.)

But life for Marilyn hardly was all glamorous romances and Hollywood feuds. Reality – sometimes sordid, sometimes quotidian – kept intruding in Marilyn's fairytale existence, as it would throughout her entire career.

For example, the unpublicized appendectomy she underwent during this period obviously frightened her – as such a procedure might well frighten many an equally thoughtful, family-oriented young woman. The note she left for her doctor was signed by Marilyn, but its sentiments seem to be vintage Norma Jeane:

'*Cut as little* as possible – I know it seems vain but doesn't really enter into it – the fact I'm a *woman* is important and means much to me.'

The typical startling, Marilyn-like detail that she taped the note to her stomach for her doctor to find before he performed the operation is probably apocryphal, perhaps an after-the-fact publicity invention. Nonetheless, the frightened young woman who penned the note was well on her way to becoming the biggest movie star in America.

When her next picture, 'Niagara' – a typical early 1950s *film noire* tale of infidelity, murder and revenge – was released, more than one critic compared Marilyn's spectacular physical attributes to those of the Falls themselves. And that was exactly how Marilyn's first dramatic starring role was advertised.

From 'Niagara' onward, Marilyn was a full-fledged star who received star billing in all of her pictures. Whitey Snyder, who at the time was escorting Marilyn to New York on weekends so she could be with Joe DiMaggio, recalls that the star treatment didn't extend to financial matters . . . at least at the beginning of the picture:

'That was her first really leading part, and she still was under a stock contract. Of course, at the end of the show they gave her a hundred-thousand dollars or something (as a bonus). But at the time she was making (the picture), she was making less than I was per week.'

Marilyn – for all the star build-up she was getting at the time – often got less than star treatment on the set. Paul A. Wurtzel, a special-effects expert who worked on a number of Marilyn's films (and whose uncle, Sol Wurtzel, came West with William Fox and became one of the earliest and most successful Fox producers), recalls a Marilyn who was not 'familiar with the crew', in the manner of many current actresses. Nonetheless . . .

He saw the man in the shadows hold her—
and kiss her! And he closed his eyes because
he was afraid to see what his wife really was!

'She never complained, and we put her through some things she could have complained about – physical things like on 'River of No Return', and when she came back from (on location at) Niagara doing her scenes on the motor launch; that was a rough picture and Mister (Henry) Hathaway was a rough director. He demanded a lot.'

Marilyn may not have been 'familiar' on her shoots, but 'Niagara' provided more than one example of the earthiness and disregard for convention that was both a part of her legend and a powerful attraction for the strait-laced American public of the 1950s. Johnny Campbell, for example, relates that on the set of 'Niagara' . . .

'There was a wardrobe gal . . . who was quite outspoken and one time she followed Marilyn out there on location in Niagara, New York, waving Marilyn's (under)pants and saying, "You can't go around without pants."'

Perhaps it was this kind of earthiness and a trouper-like attitude about her scenes once she actually was on the set that endeared her to many in the technical crews with which she worked – despite the delays and the take-upon-take perfectionism. 'Niagara' also showcased Marilyn's natural singing ability for the first time. Her one song in the picture – 'Kiss' – was written for her by Lionel Newman. He recalls that:

'MGM (which then had a record label) wanted to release a single of "Kiss" after the picture came out.

OPPOSITE PAGE: 'Niagara' was a typical early 1950s *film noire* tale of infidelity, murder and revenge. In it, Marilyn sang a song called 'Kiss'.
Copyright © Twentieth Century Fox Film Corporation

RIGHT: 'Niagara' wardrobe still of Marilyn in negligée.
Copyright © Twentieth Century Fox Film Corporation

resented, things which now would be nothing – (for example) maybe it was overly sexy when she said all she wore (to bed) was Chanel Number Five.

'So Harry Brand – Harry was the head of publicity – called me over one day . . . and he said, "Roy, will you have a talk with Marilyn? Tell her to tone down some of these sort of sexy remarks she makes, because we're getting letters from the PTA and church groups and so forth . . . complaining about this sexy posture. Just tone it down a little bit."

'And he handed me a bundle of letters, examples to show her. So I went over to her dressing room and I explained that Harry asked her to kind of tone it down just a little. And I said, "Here are some letters from different PTAs and church groups and whatnot. Harry wanted you to look at them."

'By mistake he had picked up a bunch of letters that were these obscene, dirty letters that all movie personalities get. In the mailroom, the girls that open these letters had bundled up all the dirty ones, obscene letters, which if you wanted to you could have taken up with the Postal Service to prosecute.

'So anyway, she opened up one of these letters and here was a crudely scrawled picture of a man and a woman and a (line), "Is this the way you and Joe DiMaggio look?"

'And she said, "*This* is the PTA?"

'And she opened up another one . . . from some woman saying, "What's so great about *your* bosoms?" and so on.

'And (Marilyn) said, "*This* is the Methodist Church?"'

They had a good laugh about it, Craft reports, and Marilyn did promise to make an effort to 'tone it down somewhat'.

If she did make that kind of effort, it certainly didn't extend to the screen, where soon Marilyn-as-Sex-Goddess would be on display in living colour *and* CinemaScope.

'I wanted an imprint of (Marilyn's) lips on the record. In those days, singles were very big.

'I didn't mean it to be dirty, I really didn't. (But) when they put the spindle through (the record), there would be the imprint of her lips.

'But it was provocative for the record company, although the record company was dying to do it. But in those days, they didn't take such chances . . . today it would be nothing.

'But she was willing to do it. (Marilyn) thought it was great.'

Of course, suggestive poses and *double entendres* were hardly new to Marilyn.

ABOVE: **Marilyn Monroe reading script for 'Niagara'.**
Copyright © Twentieth Century Fox Film Corporation

OPPOSITE PAGE: **'Niagara' publicity picture of Marilyn against the backdrop of the Falls.**
Copyright © Twentieth Century Fox Film Corporation

And though many of the incidents were calculated, a large number were not.

Roy Craft and others recall one event that *sounds* like a publicity plant, but which, they maintain, was not. Emphasizing that 'we were dealing with a different period than today', Craft points out that . . .

'Some of her provocative remarks were

Gentlemen Prefer Blondes

PAGES 81 TO 85 INCLUSIVE: Marilyn and Jane Russell pose for publicity stills of 'Gentlemen Prefer Blondes'. She and Russell got along splendidly, their chemistry showing both on-screen and off.

All pictures copyright © Twentieth Century Fox Film Corporation

By 1953, Marilyn was the movies' best friend. Audiences – that otherwise would stay home with Uncle Miltie – came out to theatres to see the luminous presence one columnist dubbed 'The Mmm Girl'.

'Miss Monroe looks as if she would glow in the dark,' wrote one reviewer of 'Gentlemen Prefer Blondes', in which she starred with Jane Russell.

'Gentlemen' had magic in abundance both on the set and at the box office, where it became the highest-grossing musical up to that time.

For one thing, the part of fortune-hunting Lorelei Lee was the perfect showcase for Marilyn's musical and comedic talents.

For another, she and Jane Russell got along splendidly, and their chemistry showed both on screen and off.

Darryl Zanuck himself recognized the importance of that on-screen chemistry in a September 1952 script conference, at which he emphasized how 'vital to the telling of this story' was 'Dorothy's (i.e. Russell's) real affection for Lorelei (Monroe)'.

Zanuck specified that 'we must be sold on her real affection for Lorelei or we won't be able to understand her sticking her chin out for her in the courtroom scene.' That was the scene in which Russell, in a blonde wig, impersonates her friend and even sings a parodistic reprise of 'Diamonds are a Girl's Best Friend'.

'She and Russell were like two kids,' says Walter Scott. 'It was the only time I saw Marilyn acting – I should say *re*acting – like herself, and she was having a ball.'

Continued on page 92

THIS PAGE AND OPPOSITE: Jane Russell, in blonde wig, impersonates Marilyn in the courtroom scene from 'Gentlemen Prefer Blondes'.
Both pictures copyright © Twentieth Century Fox Film Corporation

THIS PAGE AND OPPOSITE: Monroe and Russell leave their hand- and footprints in the cement at Grauman's Chinese Theatre.

THIS PAGE AND OPPOSITE: **Publicity stills of Marilyn Monroe and Jane Russell in 'Gentlemen Prefer Blondes'.**

Both copyright © Twentieth Century Fox Film Corporation

Unlike the circumstances on too many other sets, on the 'Gentlemen' set, 'we all had a mutual respect for each other,' recalls Lionel Newman. 'Maybe that's why it went so well.' In addition, he goes on:

'She loved music, she loved to be around musicians and we had a good time with her on the (recording) stage . . . More people would come on a stage when I was recording with her than when I could be recording a major dramatic picture, when you're lucky to get the musicians to show up. They used to walk through the stage – all the mailboys and delivery boys – just to get a look at her.'

Newman emphasizes that Marilyn was 'nothing but a pro with us, with music'.

Still, no set on which 'The Monroe' worked (as another columnist characterized her) could be either completely conflict- or constraint-free.

Marilyn still was the 'most professionally insecure person I ever met', as Newman describes her. And her drama coach, Natasha Lytess, still was very much on the scene, exerting an influence that one observer called 'Svengali-like'.

Of Marilyn's singing and dancing ability, Whitey Snyder – a staunch opponent of Lytess and the subsequent drama coaches – says:

'She could do it all, easy, but she wouldn't believe she could, and those damn coaches kept her down all the time; if they didn't, they would lose their jobs. At that time, they were getting about fifteen-hundred dollars a week.'

One incident on the set of 'Gentlemen' sheds interesting light on Marilyn's reputation for requiring take after take after take to 'get' a shot. They were on the recording stage, doing the painstaking sound playback for Marilyn's classic

number in that picture, 'Diamonds are a Girl's Best Friend', which Lionel Newman supervised. He remembers that . . .

'It was a difficult playback, because it was long and . . . everybody on the stage okayed it.

'I thought it was great and I told Marilyn, "Gee, one take – wonderful! – only Sinatra does that," trying to bolster her.

'She looked right through me, shaking her head negatively. And I look around and there's . . . her so-called dramatic coach . . . shaking her head (no). We had to do it again.

'Well, we made eleven takes. Finally she got on the podium with me and apologized to the orchestra, apologized to me, said I was right, the first take was the one she wanted to print.

'But that was her; she was never really sure of herself, there was always somebody putting their foot in the way.'

Continued on page 97

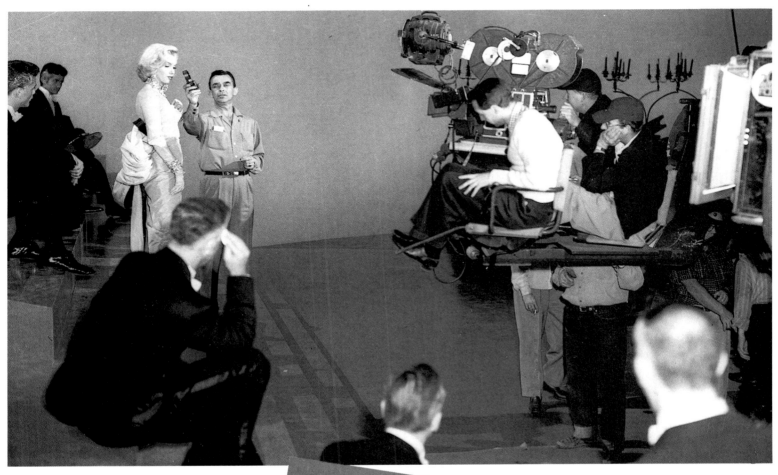

THIS PAGE AND OPPOSITE: Marilyn rehearsing her classic number, 'Diamonds are a Girl's Best Friend'.
All photographs copyright © Twentieth Century Fox Film Corporation

How To Marry A Millionaire

In the 1950s, studio chiefs at Fox and elsewhere were desperate for *anything* that would give their vanishing audiences what the home screen could not.

Sex, of course, was one possibility. Wide-screen spectacle was another.

CinemaScope was the Fox trademark name for its patented 'anamorphic' system of lens that allowed wide-screen filming and projection using standard film stock. Shortly after Fox released the first motion picture in CinemaScope, 'The Robe', a 1953 cast-of-thousands biblical spectacular, other studios followed suit with similar systems of their own (TechniScope and PanaVision, for example).

That the second CinemaScope film starred Marilyn Monroe was a stroke of casting genius. She 'fit' the process perfectly.

'How to Marry a Millionaire' also starred Betty Grable and Lauren Bacall. By all accounts, the three women got along well both on the set and off.

A number of notable moments between Marilyn and Betty Grable occurred early in the filming. 'Millionaire' marked their first pairing together and it ratified the reign of Marilyn, supplanting Betty, as Fox's new Glamour Queen.

According to Grable's biographer (*Betty Grable, the Reluctant Movie*

Queen, by Doug Warren, St Martin's Press, 1974):

'Betty saw the eclipse coming, but was philosophical about it by this time. There had always been a blonde standing by, and this time it appeared the standby was a winner.

'The crew (of "Millionaire") was . . . charged with anticipation when Grable and Monroe had their first eyeball encounter on the sound stage. Betty, fully prepared for this, chose a moment when the stage was silent, so everyone would hear her words clearly. "Honey," said Betty warmly, "I've had mine – go get yours." '

Warren relates another incident that sounds like a publicity plant but probably wasn't. Grable, who actually has a scene in the picture where she gives a manicure . . .

'. . . took one look at Marilyn's scruffy feet, and said, "You can't go before the cameras like that." Marilyn had no idea what Betty was talking about, but submitted gratefully when Betty ushered her into her dressing room to scrub and paint Marilyn's feet and toenails. Betty Grable, superstar, gave Marilyn Monroe, fledgling actress, a complete pedicure.'

Before which scene did this symbol-charged event occur? Warren alludes to 'one scene in which Marilyn

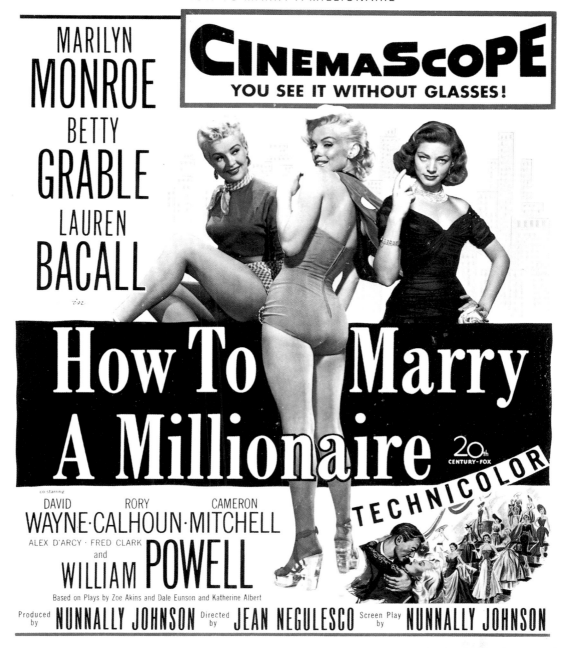

MARILYN
MONROE
BETTY
GRABLE
LAUREN
BACALL

CinemaScope
YOU SEE IT WITHOUT GLASSES!

How To Marry
A Millionaire

20th
CENTURY-FOX

TECHNICOLOR

co-starring
DAVID · RORY · CAMERON
WAYNE·CALHOUN·MITCHELL
ALEX D'ARCY · FRED CLARK
and
WILLIAM POWELL

Based on Plays by Zoe Akins and Dale Eunson and Katherine Albert

Produced by NUNNALLY JOHNSON   Directed by JEAN NEGULESCO   Screen Play by NUNNALLY JOHNSON

was to be shot from head to toe, barefooted,' but there are many possibilities.

Those who knew Grable at the time confirm both her maturity and generosity. Doubtless, she knew that the Marilyn of the 'Millionaire' period was hardly a 'fledgling', as the studio's advertising campaign for the picture makes clear.

Once again, the combination of sympathetic co-players and the right part, as the model who believes that 'men don't make passes at girls who wear glasses,' resulted in a memorable comedic performance by Marilyn. And Marilyn's critical notices (e.g. 'a deadpan

comedienne . . . as nifty as her looks') equalled her co-stars.

The picture's première had all the oldtime Hollywood glamour, and at its centre was Marilyn. Columnist Earl Leaf, a longtime Marilyn booster and friend, described the scene in an article at the time (*Movie Spotlight*, April 1954):

'Marilyn tonight was the living embodiment of every dream a young girl ever had. . . .

'Studio officials steered her towards the microphones. All afternoon Humphrey Bogart had been coaching her in what to say to the crowd. "Tell them you came to see how you loused up this picture," was his idea of a gag. *Continued on page 115*

'How To Marry A Millionaire' was the second film Fox made using its newly developed CinemaScope process.

ABOVE: 'How To Marry A Millionaire' one-sheet. Copyright © Twentieth Century Fox Film Corporation

OVERLEAF: *Action* cover of September 1953, showing Marilyn 'stretched' by Fox's newly developed CinemaScope process, and PAGE 103: Marilyn in similar pose, but 'unstretched'. Both copyright © Twentieth Century Fox Film Corporation

PAGES 104 TO 106 INCLUSIVE: Scenes from 'How To Marry A Millionaire' in which Marilyn played the model who believes that 'men aren't attentive to girls who wear glasses'. PAGE 104 (LEFT TO RIGHT): MM, Betty Grable, Lauren Bacall. PAGE 105 TOP (LEFT TO RIGHT): Lauren Bacall, David Wayne, MM. BOTTOM (LEFT TO RIGHT): Lauren Bacall, MM. PAGE 106 (LEFT TO RIGHT): Lauren Bacall and MM. All pictures copyright © Twentieth Century Fox Film Corporation

SEPTEMBER
1953

CINEMASCOPE
ON
FILM

and . .

OPPOSITE PAGE: **This wardrobe still from 'Millionaire' was not meant for publication. The comb in Marilyn's hand was the signal to the studio publicists and photographers alike that the photo was not for release.**
Copyright © Twentieth Century Fox Film Corporation

THIS PAGE AND OPPOSITE: **Marilyn posing for 'Millionaire' wardrobe stills.**

All pictures copyright © Twentieth Century Fox Film Corporation

ABOVE (LEFT TO RIGHT): **Monroe, Grable and Bacall on the set of 'How To Marry A Millionaire'.**
Copyright © Twentieth Century Fox Film Corporation

OPPOSITE PAGE: **'Millionaire' publicity still of Monroe, Bacall and Grable. By all accounts the three of them got along well both on the set and off.**
Copyright © Twentieth Century Fox Film Corporation

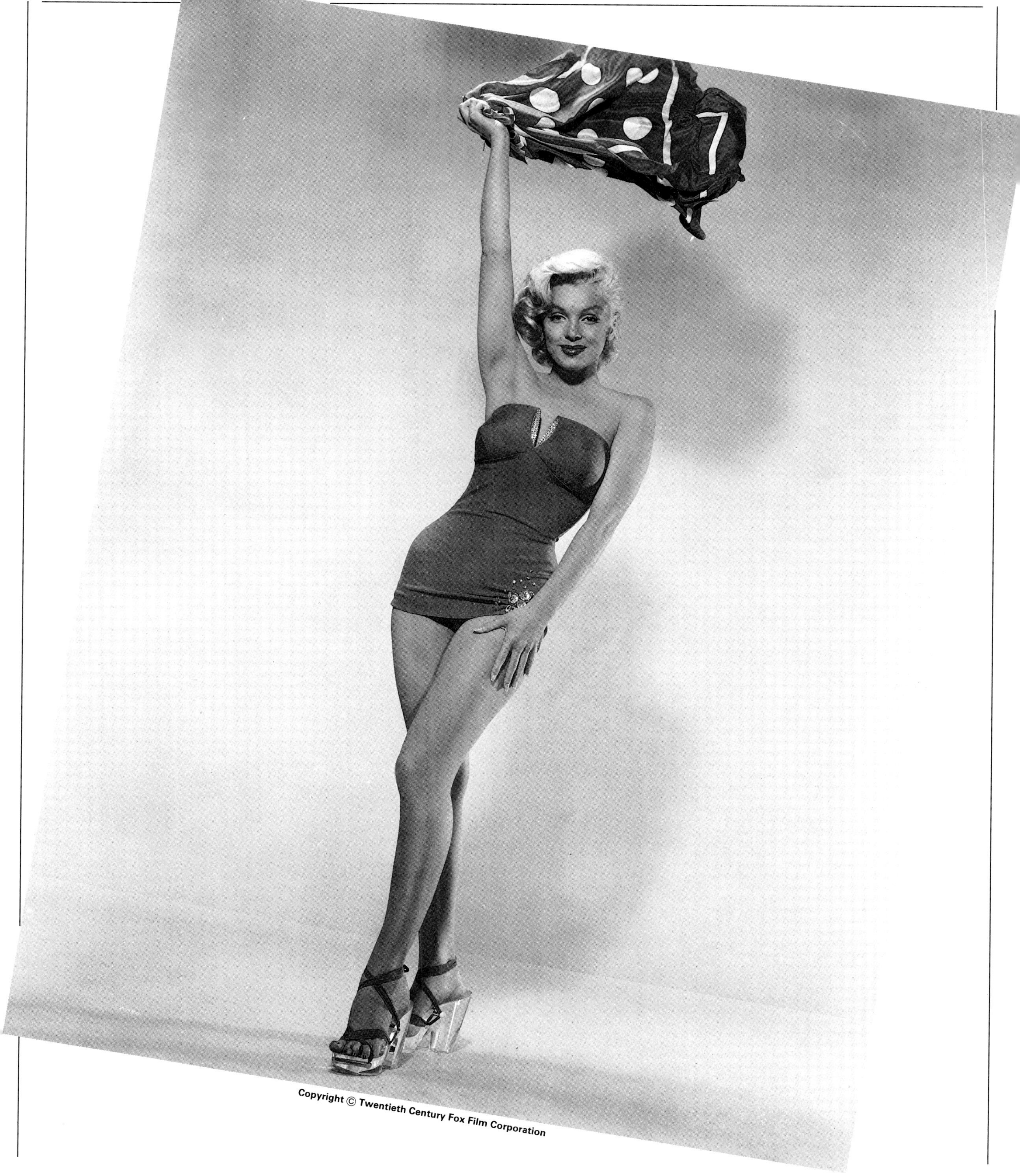

'Instead she was overcome by an impulse of beautiful simplicity and said, "I am so thrilled being at my first big première that I could almost cry!"

'Spotting the boys and girls in the fan bleachers, Marilyn launched a frontal skirmish through the cordon of policemen, reporters, columnists . . . and went directly to the stands where she began signing autographs for the fans. She's never forgotten what a film star autograph meant to her once upon a time. . . .

'Big-time stars (inside the theatre) stood on their chairs to get a glimpse of the most fabulous film star to hit Hollywood since Harlow. On some feminine faces you could see a look of green envy, or something that passed for supercilious contempt, but the collective face that turned toward Marilyn Monroe was tinged more with swoonery than snobbery.' *Continued on page 118*

OPPOSITE PAGE: The première of 'How To Marry A Millionaire' had all the oldtime Hollywood glamour and Marilyn was at its centre.
Copyright © Twentieth Century Fox Film Corporation

RIGHT: Marilyn and Nunally Johnson who wrote the screenplay and produced the film, arriving at the première.
Copyright © Twentieth Century Fox Film Corporation

ABOVE (LEFT TO RIGHT): **George Bowser (General Manager, Fox West Coast Theatres Corporation), Humphrey Bogart, Lauren Bacall, Nunally Johnson and Marilyn at the première of 'How To Marry A Millionaire'**
Copyright © Twentieth Century Fox Film Corporation

OPPOSITE PAGE: **Signing autographs for the fans at the 'Millionaire' première.**
Copyright © Twentieth Century Fox Film Corporation

The columnist also describes the 'army of studio hairdressers, make-up artists, costume experts, wardrobe mistresses and others (who) had toiled to create this masterpiece of feminine razzle-dazzle', and he adds that . . .

'I had it on good authority from a lady informant that the only garment Marilyn wore of her own was her powder-blue Nylon panties.'

The hours-long process that transformed this insecure perfectionist into a glamorous figure of mythic feminine perfection already was long-established by the time of the 'Millionaire' première.

Whitey Snyder recalls many examples of that perfectionist attitude. For example:

'She had a very slight imperfection (i.e. a tiny mole on her face). We wouldn't always put it in the same spot. Sometimes we had it on the other side.

'If we hadn't darkened it, nobody would know it was there. But she thought she could see it.'

Even now, Whitey remembers the stylized make-up that he evolved for Marilyn over the years:
'I can sit here and do the whole thing in my sleep:
'Put a base – whatever base you're using – all over, lightly.
'Then, highlight under her eyes. Pull the highlight out over and across the cheekbones to widen . . .
'Highlight her chin . . .
'Eyeshadow was toned, and that also ran out to her hairline . . .
'Then the pencil on top. Outline her eyes very clearly with pencil, but I'd make a peak right up – say almost three-sixteenths of an inch – above the pupil of her eye, and then swing it out there. And from there on out was where we put eyelashes, and then swing out past.

'Also, the bottom line was shaded in with a pencil to make her eyes stand out fully and good.
'Her eyebrows came out to a point as far as I could get them to widen her forehead. So I'd bring them to a peak just outside the centre of her eyes and then sweep down to a good-looking eyebrow. You couldn't go out much farther than that or it would look phoney.
'Shading broke the bones underneath her cheekbone. I just brought a little line down there, a little darker shadow, so that it helped her stand out.
'Lipstick, we used various colours. As the industry changed, we got down to normal colours. At first, we had a hell of a time with CinemaScope – no reds photographed anything but auburn . . . We had to go to light pink.'

ABOVE: Whitey Snyder, Marilyn's make-up man, recalls 'At first, we had a hell of a time with CinemaScope – no reds photographed anything but auburn . . . We had to go light pink.'

River Of No Return

Marilyn's co-star, Robert Mitchum, called it 'the picture of no return'. And in terms of Marilyn's career, her relationship with the studio and her personal life, it very much was.

After two big, glittery hits, she set off for Banff, Canada, and an on-location Western shoot. While Marilyn seemed to get on well with Mitchum, who helped her get through the increasingly strained filming of the picture, she was feuding with the director, Otto Preminger, over (among other matters) the presence of her drama coach on the set, as well as with the studio executives back in Hollywood. Joe DiMaggio visited her on location, and shortly after the picture's completion they were married. Then Marilyn undertook her well-publicized first boycott of the studio – honeymooning and visiting the troops in Korea, rather than acting in a picture called 'The Girl in Pink Tights'.

Script notes of the period indicate Marilyn's importance to the 'River' project. Darryl Zanuck makes the central point explicitly in an April 1953 inter-office memorandum, in which he states that:

'Unless we get a cast that is the equivalent of Robert Mitchum, Marilyn Monroe and Rory Calhoun we should not make this picture as it is basically a character and personality story.

'It will come alive only if two hot personalities like Mitchum and Monroe meet head on – then you will have fireworks but otherwise it will lay an egg in spite of the suspense, excitement and scenery.' *Continued on page 124*

Continued on page 124

BELOW: Advertising artwork of Marilyn and Robert Mitchum for 'River of No Return'. Of the film, Darryl Zanuck stated in an inter-office memorandum: '. . . It will come alive only if two hot personalities like Mitchum and Monroe meet head on – then you will have fireworks, but otherwise it will lay an egg in spite of the suspense, excitement and scenery.'
Copyright © Twentieth Century Fox Film Corporation

PAGES 122 AND 123: Mitchum, Monroe and Tommy Rettig in scenes from 'River of No Return'. All photographs copyright © Twentieth Century Fox Film Corporation

OPPOSITE PAGE: One-sheet for 'River of No Return'.
Copyright © Twentieth Century Fox Film Corporation

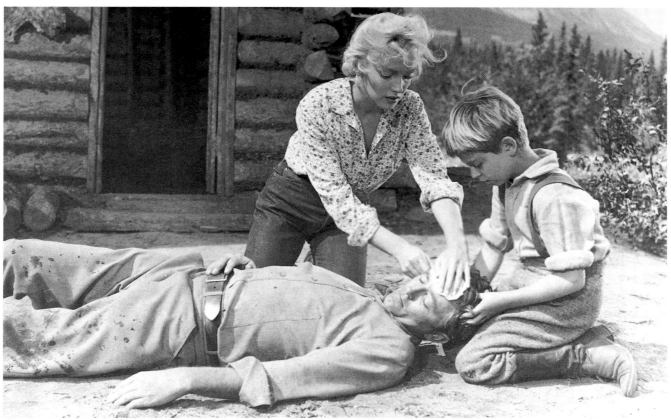

Another lengthy Zanuck memo (December 1953) that was distributed to the film's producer and writer is worth reproducing in full – both as an example of the studio chief's 'hands-on' approach to a picture that had been in production since the summer of that year, as well as of his focus and work on one of the picture's crucial scenes.

TWENTIETH CENTURY-FOX FILM CORPORATION
INTER-OFFICE CORRESPONDENCE
DATE   December 2, 1953
TO: MESSRS. RAY KLUNE   FROM   DARRYL ZANUCK
       STANLEY RUBIN
       FRANK FENTON
       JEAN NEGULESCO

SUBJECT   RIVER OF NO RETURN
Added Scenes

In analyzing the cuts which we made in the picture last night I am certain that we made a great improvement. We will have a hard-hitting tempo and this is what to expect in this type of film.

The additional scenes worked out very well with the exception of the attempted rape of Marilyn by Mitchum. We will retake this sequence again, picking it up when he first tries to kiss her. This must be a violent, aggressive scene. It is a perfect setup for such a scene and later on it will explain why Mitchum refers to himself as an animal.

We must remember that Marilyn has practically offered herself to him. He is convinced that she loves Harry (Rory Calhoun) so much that she will sleep with anyone to save Rory. This annoys the hell out of Mitchum. After all, he has lived a long time alone in the woods and she is not hard to take.

What really infuriated him is the fact that this little 'tramp' resists and repulses him. He is so sure of her invitation that he is now sore because he has made a damned fool of himself – so he decides to take it. He grabs her and kisses her; she pushes him away and socks him. It should be a real sock. She turns to run. He grabs her, jerks her back, fights her off and kisses her again. She beats at him with her hands and kicks at him, and it might be very good if she kicks him so hard in the shins that this breaks the hold and gives her a chance to break free. Maybe we could suggest that she gives him the knee in the crotch – if it is done below camera level.

As she tries to run he makes a flying leap at her and grabs her by the leg. This will, in a natural way, get them both down on the ground. He pins her down and kisses her. This is interrupted by the cry of the boy. We should feel that at this point she is utterly exhausted and that he actually would have raped her if the boy had not cried out.

I have given a great deal of thought today to the new sequence in the cave which we discussed last night. It is not only essential from the standpoint of footage but I believe it will give an amazing change of pace to the picture; it will give us a different kind of scene and it can be loaded with sex and showmanship. Audiences expect this in a picture with Marilyn Monroe and Robert Mitchum. If they don't get it they will feel that we are cheating them.

The new sequence will come after Marilyn faints on the raft, following the end of the shooting of the rapids in the gorge.

Here is the scene as I see it:

DISSOLVE IN: INT. CAVE, shooting out through the mouth of the cave. This can be late afternoon, not too long after Marilyn has fainted. At a distance we see Mitchum coming up the hill as if he is coming up from the river, which is apparently below them and not visible at this point. He is carrying Marilyn in his arms. Both are still dripping wet. The Boy follows behind them. He is carrying the pack with the blankets in it, and probably the ax. We want to give the impression that this is probably only a hundred yards from the river. They have spotted the cave and are climbing up towards it. As they walk towards us Mitchum and the Boy constantly look from side to side, on the alert for Indians.

Marilyn is conscious but she is in the grip of a chill. She trembles, her teeth chatter, and she looks completely spent. Mitchum has probably had to wade ashore with her in his arms.

As they pause at the mouth of the cave Mitchum tells the Boy: 'Stay here. Keep your eyes open. If you see or hear anything – whistle.'

The Boy crouches down and turns to look down the hill as Mitchum carries Marilyn into the cave. He selects a spot and puts her down. She can't control her shivering. Mitchum gets the blankets out of the pack and says to Marilyn, 'We can't light a fire until we're sure there are no Indians around – or until it gets dark. Get out of your clothes and wrap yourself in these blankets.'

Marilyn nods. She bends down to take off her boots. Probably we can get some business out of Mitchum removing the boots which are soaked with water. He does the gag of turning around, back to her, holding her leg between his own two legs, gripping the boot and asking her to push with her other foot because the boot is water-soaked and hard to remove.

When the boots are off Mitchum looks at her and says, 'I'll wait outside. Dry yourself with one of the blankets and wrap yourself in the other.'

He goes out of the cave as Marilyn, still weak and exhausted, starts to unbutton her dress.

At the mouth of the cave we play a scene between Mitchum and the Boy. We must remember that at this point in the story there is a strained attitude between them. The Boy has learned that his father shot a man in the back. We must have the feeling that the boy's sympathy at this point is entirely with Marilyn. During the following scene Mitchum and the Boy speak in whispers.

ABOVE: 'Marilyn nods. She bends down to take off her boots. Probably we can get some business out of Mitchum removing the boots which are soaked with water. He does the gag of turning around, back to her, holding her leg between his own two legs, gripping the boot and asking her to push with her other foot because the boot is water-soaked and hard to remove . . .'
Darryl Zanuck visualising the above scene from 'River of No Return' in a memo of December 1953 that was distributed to the film's producer and writer.
Copyright © Twentieth Century Fox Film Corporation

BOY
Is she going to die?

MITCHUM
No . . . She's a strong girl. That type doesn't die easily.

BOY
But she is very sick, isn't she?

MITCHUM
She's sick – but not too sick. Chill – exhaustion – and hunger.

BOY
(*looking around*)
Will we have to stay here long?

MITCHUM
Not too long – *we're* hungry, too.
(*after a pause*)
You go ahead and scrape up some firewood. Maybe some pine knots. When it gets dark we'll take a chance on building a fire in the cave.

The boy starts away.

MITCHUM
(*calling after him*)
Be as quiet as you can – and keep your eyes open.

The boy nods, and exits.

MARILYN'S VOICE
(o.s.)
I have the blanket on.

Mitchum turns and goes into the cave. Marilyn is curled up on the ground. She still looks blue, still shivers. Her wet clothes are in a heap beside her. Mitchum picks them up, one by one, wrings them out and spreads them out on a ledge, or possibly on a bush which is growing inside the cave. Marilyn watches him in silence as he wrings out each garment. The last one is her lace-edged drawers. Up to now

Mitchum has been expressionless, but after he hangs up the drawers he looks at them and says,

MITCHUM
(*in a dry voice*)
Pretty fancy for the Northwest.

MARILYN
(*giving him a cold eye*)
The Emporium – in Kansas City.

Mitchum turns to face her, sees that once again she is having a fit of the shakes. Serious and businesslike, he orders:

MITCHUM
Turn over on your stomach and stretch out, face down.

She looks at him for a moment, then complies. He kneels beside her. The blanket is tucked around her. He starts to massage her; first the back of her neck, then her shoulders, then her arms, and then down her back. There is no sex in this; Mitchum is completely professional as he goes about the business of increasing her circulation. But at least we, the audience, know that she is naked under the blanket, and that they are close together. Mitchum pauses, puts his hand on her forehead.

MITCHUM
(*after he sees that her forehead is not fevered*)
No need to worry. It's mostly the cold water, the shock, and exhaustion.

MARILYN
A thick T-bone steak wouldn't do any harm.

MITCHUM
I'd settle for a squirrel.

He starts to massage her again. After a moment:

MARILYN
I'm sorry I opened my big mouth in front of the boy. . . . You hurt me and I wanted to hurt you back.

Mitchum doesn't answer. Then he hears a sound out of scene, stops, quickly reaches for the ax. He relaxes as the Boy enters, carrying an armful of firewood and a dead quail. He puts down the firewood, and holds the quail out for Mitchum to see.

BOY
I hit it with a stone!

MITCHUM
(*taking it*)
It's not much – but beggars can't be choosers.

(If it fits the mood of the scene, we might have a reaction from Marilyn, or the Boy, or both – another of those old sayings of Mitchum's!)

Mitchum takes out his knife to slit the quail.

MITCHUM
(*to the Boy*)
See anything?

BOY
Nothing.

MITCHUM
We'll make a fire the minute it gets dark.

DISSOLVE TO:
INT. CAVE – NIGHT. The only light is the faint glow from the fire which has almost burned itself out. The clothes are dry. The Boy is sound asleep close to the dying fire. Mitchum sits facing the mouth of the cave. Marilyn, still curled up in the blanket, is near the fire.

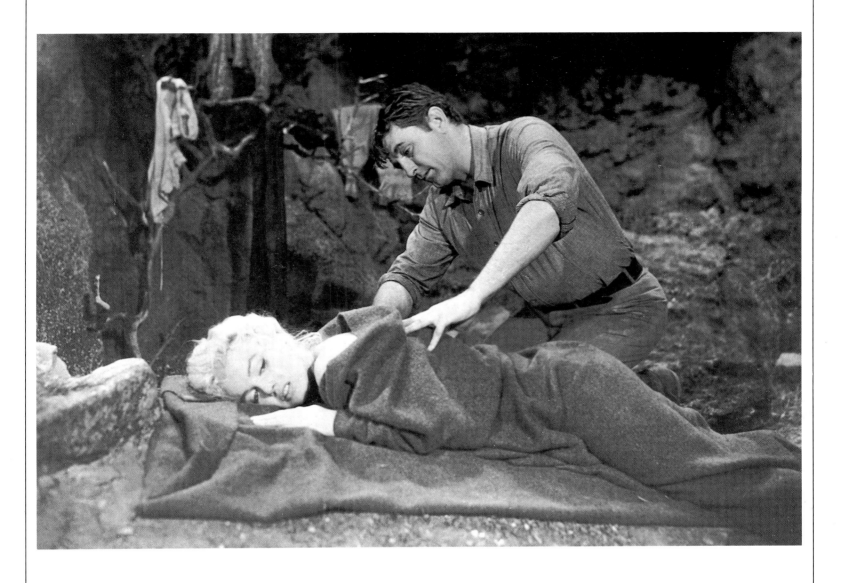

ABOVE: This scene between Monroe and
Mitchum in 'River of No Return' was mentioned
by Zanuck in his December 1953 memo:
'. . . The blanket is tucked around her. He starts
to massage her; first the back of her neck, then
her shoulders, then her arms, and then down
her back. There is no sex in this; Mitchum is
completely professional as he goes about the
business of increasing her circulation. But at
least we, the audience, know that she is naked
under the blanket, and that they are close
together . . .'

MARILYN
(*to Mitchum, in a half-whisper*)
If it wasn't for me you'd be half way to Council City by now.

MITCHUM
(*grimly*)
If it wasn't for Weston I'd be sleeping in a bunk at the cabin.

He gets up, walks over to the mouth of the cave, stands there looking out. Marilyn raises up on one elbow, looks at him. As she raises up, this natural movement pulls the blanket down, exposing one bare shoulder.

MARILYN
Can't you get some sleep?

Mitchum turns around and looks at her. We have a point of view shot – Mitchum looking at her bare shoulder. There is no reaction from him whatever.

MITCHUM
I can – but it wouldn't be safe. Sometimes Indians can smell smoke farther than they can see it.

Marilyn lies back, draws the blanket up, covering her shoulder. Mitchum turns back to the mouth of the cave, stares

out. On this we DISSOLVE TO:

INT. CAVE – several hours later, probably just before dawn. Mitchum is sitting at the mouth of the cave, fighting to keep awake. Marilyn is asleep, still curled up by the fire which is practically out by now. The Boy awakens, gets up quietly and goes over to Mitchum at the mouth of the cave.

ABOVE: Marilyn and Tommy Rettig in cave scene from 'River of No Return'.

MITCHUM

It'll be light in another hour – and we can get moving.

BOY

Didn't you sleep at all?
(*Mitchum shakes his head*)
Let me watch. I'll wake you up when it's light.

Before Mitchum can reply there is a noise. Mitchum and the Boy tense, and we play this for suspense as Mitchum reaches for the ax and motions to the Boy to get back out of sight. They wait, listening intently. Again the noise – a kind of crackling noise which might be made by someone coming stealthily through the brush. The noise ceases, and again there is silence. Then it starts again. Mitchum stands to one side, the ax raised, ready to fell whoever enters. The Boy, wide-eyed, crouches in the background. Marilyn sleeps on. Now the noise is a little closer. We Cut To:

EXT. CAVE. We see nothing. It is hazy dawn and if there is someone hiding in the trees we can't see them. But again we hear the crackling noise in the bushes as if someone is creeping closer. It might be an animal; it might be Indians, on hands and knees. But it is certainly something. When we have milked this for all possible suspense, suddenly a pair of raccoons come out of the dimness and into the circle of light at the mouth of the cave.

Mitchum, inside the cave, has stepped back from the mouth of the cave and is poised to one side, the ax upraised, ready to spring on the intruder. Presently the two raccoons amble to the mouth of the cave, peer in. Mitchum, stunned, lowers the ax. Then he realizes that here is breakfast, and raising the ax he springs towards the raccoons. But they are too fast for him, and they scamper out of the cave and off into the dawn. The noise has awakened Marilyn, and she sits up with a start.

MARILYN

What was it?

MITCHUM

(*chagrined*)
Our breakfast . . . It just left.

                    DISSOLVE TO:

The scene already photographed, of the raft in calm water: Mitchum is sound asleep, Marilyn and the Boy operate the boat. A few minutes later Marilyn speaks the line: 'I don't know what happened to me back there. I just passed out.'

I would like you to polish these scenes and I want to shoot them as quickly as they can be written and prepared. If possible, I would like to have these scenes polished by Frank Fenton so that when we see the picture again Monday night we will know exactly what we are going to shoot within the next couple of days.

I am completely sold on the above. It fits into the pattern of our picture. It develops the relationship between our characters and it plugs a couple of holes where we have previously made eliminations. Moreover, it is the kind of showmanship sequence which belongs in this picture.   D.F.Z.

That cave scene and a number of others were shot back in Hollywood, on the set, long after the on-location travails had ended. Special-effects expert Paul Wurtzel was one of those who did not go out on location:

'I was doing "King of the Khyber Rifles" at the time. But when ("River") came back to the studio, we had to do a lot of close-ups and pick-up shots for which we used the cyclorama (a curved backdrop used usually to simulate outdoor sky).

'She was coming down the rapids with the rough water and the arrows being shot at her, and it would have been impossible to do on a practical location because they had no control. Here we

had control because we could bounce the raft around the rapid waters and throw the wake over her, plus have accuracy in shooting the arrows in on wires . . .'

'River' was also known as a rough picture with a rough director, Wurtzel remembers. And during the on-location shooting, he says, 'I think they all knew they had a star blossoming out there.'

Of the most famous 'River' on-location incident, there are a number of versions. In her autobiography *Shelley: Also Known as Shirley* (Ballantine, 1980), Marilyn's close friend and one-time roommate, Shelley Winters, recalls visiting the Canadian location on a difficult day when director Otto Preminger . . .

'. . . began to use dreadful language, implying to an imaginary friend that he had to use her in this picture because of pressure from the entire board of directors of Twentieth Century Fox and that she was so untalented she should stick to her original "profession".'

When Marilyn's public humiliation finally was over, Winters reports, she led her friend away to a waiting limousine . . .

'. . . she slipped a little as we walked toward the limousine. . . . I caught her other arm as she slipped and just to make conversation, I said something like: "Watch your step, you can break a leg on this wet slippery pier." We both got into the limousine. . . . When we arrived, I got out first, but Marilyn stayed where she was and said "I can't get out I've broken my leg."'

Zanuck was called, medical specialists were flown out from Hollywood. The verdict was a sprain, but Marilyn insisted on crutches and a walking cast to the knee.

When she hobbled back to the set, Winters says, she found a different Otto Preminger: 'If he had dared say one word out of line to this poor crippled girl, the crew would have torn him limb from limb, and he knew it.'

Winters remembers that that night she and Marilyn went dancing.

Whitey Snyder, who, of course, was also on location for 'River' remembers it differently. Marilyn was shooting a scene that required her to walk out to a raft that was tied about six feet in the water; as she started out, she tripped on an underwater rock. He was close by, he says, when . . .

'. . . she fell, spraining her ankle in the river, and I pulled her out.

'I used to have to carry her around on my back . . . for a week or so. Put her in one spot or another spot on the set, carry her up to the car when we were done.

'If we were shooting down the hill, I'd pack her down, pack her back. A couple of guys would say, "Gee, let me do that." 'She'd say, "No, I trust him, he's got a strong back."' *Continued on page 132*

OPPOSITE PAGE (ABOVE): **Marilyn, Mitchum and Rettig under Indian attack in the studio. This 'River of No Return' scene, with arrows being shot at the cast, had to be done in the studio because it would have been impossible to control on location.**

OPPOSITE PAGE (BELOW): **'River of No Return' raft scene shot on location.**

RIGHT: **Marilyn on crutches after the famous 'River' on-location incident.**

Making-up Marilyn for 'River' presented an unusual challenge, Whitey says. He had to 'make her more plain . . . a little more outdoorish, which was hard to do with her.'

The outdoor look was difficult, the plain was not. As Whitey and a number of others testify, when Marilyn wasn't 'on' – that is, when she wasn't inhabiting her public persona of Marilyn Monroe, Dreamgirl and Sex Goddess – she preferred to inhabit blue jeans and would let herself look something less than presentable.

For example, on location for 'River', Whitey remembers one night when . . .

'. . . she and I and a couple of other people were staying up in a motel about eight miles out of town.

'She had her face full of grease – she wanted to protect her skin – and she wanted to go to town, to walk around.

'And I said, "Nope, not unless you wash your face . . . I don't want to be seen with you."

'That was her whole life, trying to keep everything perfect. I knew why she'd do it, but I had to give her a little hell every once in a while . . .'

But despite everything that happened on that set, this still was Marilyn Ascendant, soon to become the wife of the most famous baseball player in the country.

And no amount of make-up or grease could hide – and no amount of professional grief could diminish – her natural, guileless exuberance.

RIGHT AND OPPOSITE PAGE: Two wardrobe stills of Marilyn in profile (the comb is an indication that these photos were not originally intended for publication). According to Whitey Snyder, making up Marilyn for 'River' presented an unusual challenge. He had to 'make her look more plain . . . a little more outdoorish, which was hard to do with her'.

Both photographs courtesy Allan Snyder

ABOVE AND OPPOSITE PAGE: Two publicity stills of
Marilyn in 'River of No Return'.
Both copyright © Twentieth Century Fox Film Corporation

There's No Business Like Show Business

Irony abounds in the title of Marilyn's next picture. Starring along with Marilyn in this musical 'tribute' to composer Irving Berlin were Ethel Merman, Donald O'Connor, Dan Dailey, Mitzi Gaynor and Johnny Ray.

For one thing, Marilyn spent the first quarter of 1954 on suspension (and on honeymoon). She and new husband Joe DiMaggio toured the Far East, where Marilyn's visits with the soldiers in Korea sparked a number of near riots. When she finally returned to the Fox lot for 'Show Business', it was with a new seven-year contract. But it wouldn't be long before both the contract and her marriage were broken.

For another thing, despite her star billing and her adamance about not appearing in 'Pink Tights', she returned to do a picture that was far from distinguished (although it certainly aspired to be) and in which she had a relatively small part. In fact, in all but the final versions of the script (by Nora and Henry Ephron), no mention is made of Marilyn's character or that she would play the part. And, in a memorandum to Irving Berlin about the proposed film, Darryl Zanuck's listing of his 'ideal cast' doesn't even include Ethel Merman; Zanuck expressed the hope that actress Jane Wyman would play the part of the show business family's matriarch.

Later, interestingly enough, director Sol Siegel suggested (in a February 1953 note to the Ephrons) that Ethel Merman should have the 'Heat Wave' song, which would be just right for her.

That song, of course, became one of the classic Monroe musical numbers.

She had conflicts, once again, on the set, but, as Lionel Newman puts it, 'some of the people she had troubles with, we all had troubles with.'

And, once again, she got along well with her fellow leading lady. As Roy Craft remembers, 'Ethel (Merman) was an old pro and got along with her fine.'

By this time, too, Marilyn had a small, albeit trusted, professional family on whom she could call, particularly for song-and-dance numbers.

One of those was famed choreographer Jack Cole, with whom she first worked on 'Gentlemen Prefer Blondes'.

Another was her vocal coach, for whom she showed great affection; among her intimates at that time, it was generally understood that Marilyn and her vocal coach were having an affair. The affair ended when he attempted suicide because of Marilyn, or, he attempted suicide because the affair had ended – accounts differ; there is agreement, however, on the fact that Marilyn held a vigil by his bedside while he was recovering from the attempt.

Her vocal coach, one informed observer said, 'stylized her – her phrasing, her whole approach to a song.' Her inimitable rendition of 'Heat Wave'

Continued on page 147

LEFT AND BELOW: Marilyn on the set of 'There's No Business Like Show Business'.
Both photographs copyright © Twentieth Century Fox Film Corporation

PAGES 141 TO 143 INCLUSIVE: Marilyn entertains in 'There's No Business Like Show Business', in which she plays the Broadway-bound hat-check girl who joins the act of a vaudeville family.
All photographs copyright © Twentieth Century Fox Film Corporation

was due to his 'teaching her how to phrase it, the right way to breathe'.

Marilyn was much less temperamental than most artists with whom he worked, says Lionel Newman, who emphasizes her complete professionalism, as well as the perfectionism that plagued her and was marred by her insecurity and her dependence on her coaches. Her single display of temper, he recalls, involved her vocal coach:

'She was not at all temperamental with us, with me. I only had one incident that happened while I was doing "There's No Business Like Show Business".

'They were all Irving Berlin tunes. My brother Alfred did part of them, but I did all of Marilyn's songs.

'And when Irving Berlin came to LA, he was on our recording stage and he wanted to hear the numbers.

'He was ecstatic about them. He was complimentary to me. He couldn't believe that Marilyn did her own singing, which she did; there wasn't one note ever that was looped or dubbed for her.

'Well, we had a boy . . . who was our pianist . . . and he was wonderful. And Marilyn was very devoted to him and grateful to him, because he was . . . her "vocal coach". So she was incensed that I didn't call (him) over. It was just one of those things, that you don't call everybody over who had anything to do with the picture, because Irving wanted to hear them.

'So she chewed my tail out and said unless Irving went over to (his) bungalow and apologized and told him personally how good he thought it was, she wouldn't come back to record with us.

'So I told her in my Oxford English, I said, **** you, I'm not going to take this **** from you, Marilyn. And I was really teed off at her, I said, you let my brother finish the picture with you.

'And I stormed out of my own office, and she was left there. And I was incensed because I told her it wasn't I who had done it . . .

'Anyway, Irving did go the next day to see (him) to tell him how much he thought of his vocal coaching and vocal arrangements for Marilyn. And the next day she came in very sheepishly and apologized to me.

'She was very loyal, ridiculously loyal – too loyal. She sometimes forgot what was involved. That was typical of Marilyn.'

BELOW AND PAGES 148 AND 149: Donald O'Connor, Mitzi Gaynor, Marilyn and various cast and crew members on the set of 'There's No Business Like Show Business'.

BELOW: Grand finale from 'There's No Business Like Show Business'. Left to right: Johnny Ray, Mitzi Gaynor, Dan Dailey, Ethel Merman, Donald O'Connor, Marilyn Monroe.

The Seven Year Itch

In real life, Marilyn Monroe never even got close to reaching the Seven Year Itch-stage in her marriage to former Yankee baseball star Joe DiMaggio.

By most accounts, Marilyn and Joe's marital problems crystallized during the 'Itch' filming of Marilyn's single most famous screen scene. According to many depictions of that event, the repeated two a.m. exposure of his wife's panties before a cheering crowd of New Yorkers – in the on-location filming of the skirt-billowing scene – so unnerved and incensed the puritanical DiMaggio that the marriage ended there and then.

However, Roy Craft, who was there, remembers it differently. The week in New York City had been pandemonium from the very beginning.

'The Russians could have flown over the airport when we landed and no one would have noticed,' he says. The huge crowds eager for a glimpse of Marilyn were just a foretaste of what he remembers as 'a real frantic and enjoyable time, because everything broke our way . . .

'We were staying at the St Regis (hotel), as I recall. I hardly got out of my room, because my room was the press headquarters and the calls were coming in in shifts – morning editions (of newspapers) calling in late at night and the afternoon editions early in the morning and so forth . . .

'We were on the front pages constantly and anything she did was front-page news . . .

'The skirt-blowing episode was fantastic. This was Lexington Avenue, as I remember, and the scene was a very simple scene (in which Marilyn) had gone with Tom Ewell to one of these monster films. And they come out after the show . . . and she's standing over a grating and she says she feels sorry for that poor monster or something. And then a subway train goes rumbling underneath and blows her skirt up.

'The production crew had picked this Lexington Avenue newsreel theatre, which they had in those days – the crew had picked this one because at two in the morning the street is entirely deserted and we'd have no problem. So they re-dressed the theatre with this monster movie and so forth.

'Well, I helped leak the story – and (Walter) Winchell had it – that Marilyn was going to be on Lexington Avenue at two in the morning. So they had one of the biggest crowds ever . . . There were all the working press – the real photographers – plus all the amateurs.

'So when the scene starts, all these flashbulb cameras were going off . . . pop, pop, pop and, my God, you couldn't do anything. Finally, I stepped out and said to the working press, "Fellahs, will you tell this bunch to calm down and not shoot? Let them get the scene, then (Billy Wilder) the director says he'll re-do –

move the big cameras out of the way – so that everybody can get real good pictures of Marilyn and Tom.'

'Well, they did that, finally got the shot, then moved the cameras, then everybody starts shooting . . . That was the night that Joe DiMaggio and (columnist) Winchell came, and he was reported as saying he disapproved of Marilyn showing her legs and that sort of thing, which I don't think was true.

'I think it was a made-up quote. I never heard him say it and I don't think he (ever) did say it. He was quoted as saying he was irate and what not, but when he had married her she was a major personality and a sex symbol and he knew what he was getting into . . .

'Joe was very much in love with her, but at the time we went back there (to New York), they were already in the process of breaking up. It was after they got back (to Los Angeles) that the final break was made. That was a spectacle in itself . . .'

Craft was a witness to that final spectacle, too. It occurred back in Los Angeles, where in-studio filming of 'Itch' was scheduled to resume . . .

'We got a call from the press saying Marilyn had announced she would be at her (celebrity) attorney's office at nine o'clock the next morning for a press conference.

'So I went down to (publicity director) Harry Brand's office and said, "My God, Harry, Marilyn can't have a press conference. She shouldn't have a press conference. What could she say? She can't make dirty cracks about Joe, everybody loves Joe. You can't have a press conference unless you're going to say something. Why don't we just tell the

ABOVE (LEFT TO RIGHT): Director Billy Wilder, Marilyn and co-star Tom Ewell working on the subway grate scene in 'The Seven Year Itch'.
Copyright © Twentieth Century Fox Film Corporation

PAGES 154 AND 155: Marilyn's famous skirt billowing episode is captured in this poster for 'The Seven Year Itch'.
Both copyright © Twentieth Century Fox Film Corporation

Continued on page 156

press that she's just leaving for work at ten o'clock in the morning as usual?"

'Well, we got together with (her attorney) and worked it out that she would not have a regular press conference, but she would see the press as she left for work.

'Now, they had a house in Beverly Hills, and Joe was still there. He was on the second floor and she was on the first or something.

'But anyway, that morning, in anticipation of her seeing the press en route to work, the studio sent the hairdresser and the make-up man and the works over. And the press started gathering.

'They were all over the lawn and in the trees and everywhere else. Then finally, here came a black Cadillac that drew up, and it was Joe's buddy from San Francisco. And then (Marilyn's attorney) arrived and he went in. Harry Brand arrived and he went in . . .

'And the tension starts mounting . . . At long last, here came out Joe, with his buddy carrying his suitcase. They got pictures of that . . . And they asked him, "Where you going, Joe?" And he said, "I'm going home." And, "Where's your home, Joe?" And he said, "San Francisco has always been my home." And they got a picture of Joe waving and the Cadillac (leaving).

'Then the suspense begins building again. And finally, the door opens and here comes Marilyn out the front door, with Harry Brand on one arm and (her attorney) on the other. And she comes out and the newsreels and the radio and everybody starts going forward, and (columnist) Sheila Graham kicked one of the newspaper guys in the pants for getting in her way. There was a big scramble.

'But anyway, Marilyn comes out and they all rush up and they put microphones in her face – "Give us a statement, Marilyn!"

'And she says, "I can't, I can't." And

then she kind of collapsed.

'And Harry and (her attorney) sort of helped her to her car. And she looked pale and wan and absolutely beautiful . . .'

The photographers snapped pictures of Marilyn 'waving a sad farewell' as the car drove her off to the studio, Craft recalls. Within days, the star with a reputation for being unable to meet shooting schedules was back on Sound Stage Nine, on the Fox lot, doing retakes on 'The Seven Year Itch'.

'That's where I gained my notoriety,' special-effects man Paul Wurtzel recalls with a smile. Although the skirt-billowing scene already had been done once on-location in New York, soundtrack and other problems made it necessary to build a mock-up of the New York theatre on Sound Stage Nine and do re-takes.

That's when Wurtzel got to do the job that thousands of other men gladly would have paid to do. He stood below the mock-up subway grate and operated the air machine simulating a passing train . . .

'It was a real hurry-up deal,' says Wurtzel, recalling that director Billy Wilder was trying to catch up on the shooting schedule. 'I got a call to come in on a Saturday . . .

'There was a cue light down there (beneath the "grate") and as the subway was supposed to be passing underneath creating a draft and blowing up her skirt, I would get one cue light, open up the blower we had funnelled in there . . .

'And when they gave me the second cue light, I'd shut it down, (which) meant the train had already passed . . .

'We went on all day. I do recall (that) Marilyn, when she was lined up for the shot, she'd squat down and there I'd be, looking up at Marilyn and, you know, we'd be talking to one another – "How's everything going?" and "Too bad you

have to do the scene over again and over again" – we were a good six hours until Billy Wilder got what he wanted . . .

'Not realizing what the later publicity would be from it, I thought it was just another assignment – a hell of a nice assignment. The only thing I got out of it (then) was a cinder fell in my eye, but we got that out eventually . . .'

The picture itself turned out to be one of Marilyn's few unqualified successes, where all the myriad movie-making elements came together perfectly – cast, director, crew and script. And Marilyn was the ideal embodiment of the script's nameless 'Girl Upstairs'.

Continued on page 160

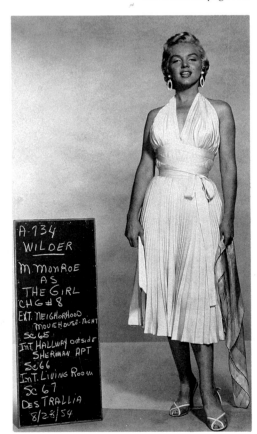

ABOVE: Marilyn poses for wardrobe still in subway grate costume.

OPPOSITE PAGE (BOTTOM): The man under the grate – special effects expert Paul Wurtzel.

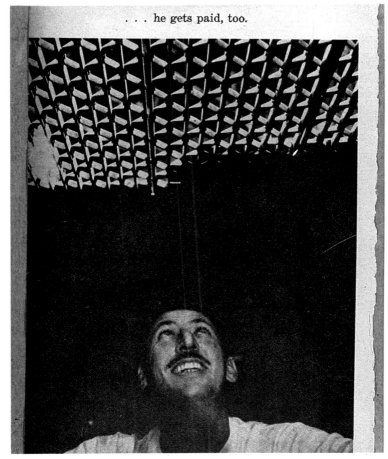

. . . he gets paid, too.

The literate Billy Wilder–George Axelrod screenplay even came with in-jokes. For example, early in the film, Tom Ewell says self-confidently that . . . 'Some husbands think that because their wives are away for the summer, they can just run wild – do any terrible thing they want.'

And he mentions one such husband, whose wife hadn't been gone two days when he went out and got himself tattooed. That particular husband just happened to have the same name as the screen writer of 'Gentlemen Prefer Blondes' – Charles Lederer (called 'Charlie Lederer' in the script).

Later, Ewell is rebuked by his wife, who tells him that . . . 'Lately you've begun to imagine in CinemaScope – with Stereophonic Sound' . . . which, of course, is a reference to Fox's own new trademarked process. And still farther on in the script, there is the following dialogue between RICHARD (Ewell) and TOM (Sonny Tufts):

RICHARD: I'll fight it in every court in the country. Because I can explain everything. The stairs. The cinnamon toast. The blonde in the kitchen.

TOM: Now, wait a minute, Dickie-boy. Let's just take it easy. What blonde in the kitchen?

RICHARD: Well, wouldn't you like to know. Maybe it's Marilyn Monroe.

TOM: Drunk. Blind, stinking drunk – at eight-thirty in the morning.

And, of course, the blonde in the kitchen *was* Marilyn Monroe.

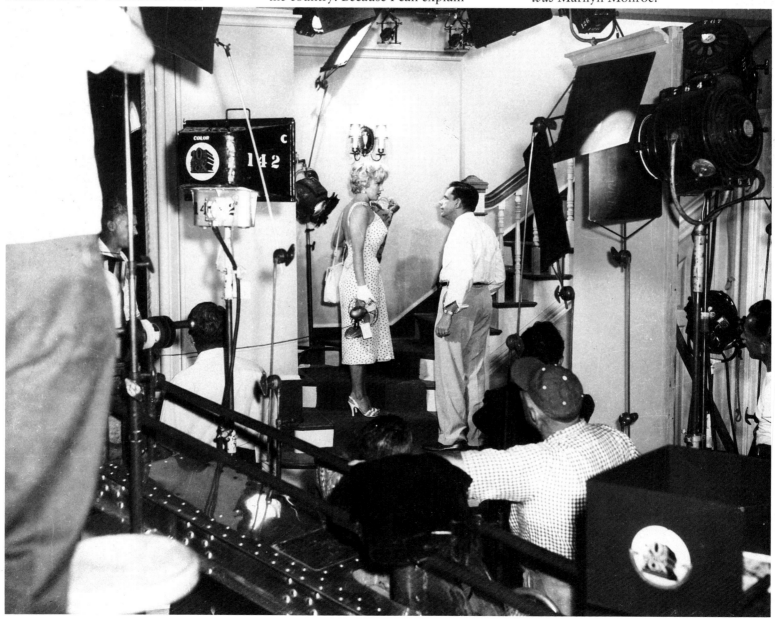

All photographs copyright © Twentieth Century Fox Film
Corporation

ABOVE AND OPPOSITE PAGE: Bathtub scene from 'The
Seven Year Itch'. The lucky man wrestling with
the plumbing is Victor Moore.
**Both photographs copyright © Twentieth Century Fox Film
Corporation**

Bus Stop

Marilyn Monroe's life changed in several ways between the end of 'The Seven Year Itch' and the start of her next picture, 'Bus Stop'. Many of those changes were for the better; a few, tragically, were not.

More than a year went by between the two films. During that time, she resumed her public feud with the studio, which accused her of breaking her contract.

Marilyn refused to appear in a picture called 'How to be Very, Very Popular'. Instead, she moved to New York, where she formed her own production company (in partnership with photographer Milton Greene), enrolled in Lee Strasberg's Actors' Studio (US temple of the Stanislavski Method), began analysis and was courted by (or courted, according to some accounts) playwright Arthur Miller, who was in the process of divorce and whom she would marry following the completion of the Joshua Logan film of William Inge's play.

When the legal entanglements with the studio were finally resolved, Marilyn returned to Hollywood with a new contract that allowed outside films. Her first Fox project was 'Bus Stop', in which she played Cherie, the second-rate saloon singer who attracts the naïve, hot-blooded young cowboy (Don Murray).

In an interview with columnist Louella Parsons (*L.A. Examiner*, 4/15/56) following 'Bus Stop', Marilyn went to some lengths to deny the reality of the Fox feud. She said that she owed her big break at Twentieth Century Fox to Darryl Zanuck, and although he was angry with her when she would not do 'Pink Tights' and 'How to be Very, Very Popular', that was no different from the way he would have been with anyone else in the same situation. She also said that the rumours of a feud between herself and the Twentieth Century Fox studios were completely untrue.

However, studio publicity notes of the time offering 'Vital Statistics on "Bus Stop"', sound a note of suggestive ambivalence about Marilyn's return to the fold. She was bringing with her a new drama coach . . .

'Much has been made in the public prints of the "new" Marilyn Monroe, and while it is true that her 14-month vacation from films while studying with the famed Actors' Studio in New York has given her a new poise and confidence, it is also true that Marilyn is still Marilyn, as evidenced by the excitement created in the studio commissary whenever Marilyn made one of her infrequent appearances.

'Helping her with her interpretation of the character of Cherie, a rather naïve little "floozy" who would like to live the good life, was Paula Strassberg (sic), wife of Lee Strassberg (sic), director of the studio which has turned out so many famous actors, and mother of Susan Strassberg (sic) the sensational star of

ABOVE: Scene from 'Bus Stop'.
Copyright © Twentieth Century Fox Film Corporation

OPPOSITE PAGE (TOP): Director of 'Bus Stop', Josh Logan, and Marilyn.

OPPOSITE PAGE (BELOW): Marilyn framed against the snow in this publicity shot for 'Bus Stop'. Special effects expert Paul Wurtzel remembers the film for 'the new snow machines that spewed out (soap) detergent for falling snow and almost took the paint off everything'.
Both photographs copyright © Twentieth Century Fox Film Corporation

PAGES 172 AND 173: One of the most famous moments in 'Bus Stop' – Marilyn's rendition of 'That Old Black Magic'.
All photographs copyright © Twentieth Century Fox Film Corporation

"The Diary of Anne Frank" on Broadway.

'Mrs Strassberg worked closely with Miss Monroe during the production, and certain wags have suggested – remembering the famous slogan, "Garbo Speaks" – that the studio ballyhoo "Bus Stop" with the line, "Marilyn Acts!"

'However, those who remember the blonde glamour girl in "Seven Year Itch", "How to Marry a Millionaire" and "Gentlemen Prefer Blondes", insist that despite her legendary naïveté, Marilyn has been a very fine actress all along.'

This oddly dismissive encomium, it should be noted, was about a role for which many Hollywood observers thought Marilyn deserved at least an Academy Award nomination. (The Oscar that year went to Ingrid Bergman for 'Anastasia', another Fox picture.) The critics, too, generally found Marilyn's acting to be a revelation, and director Logan (who had worked with Stanislavski) had nothing but praise for her:

'Marilyn was a totally satisfying professional during all the (on-location) shooting in Phoenix,' Logan says in his autobiography (*Movie Stars, Real People, and Me*; Delacorte Press, 1978). 'She was always on time.'

Logan designed one of the most famous moments in the picture – Marilyn's rendition of 'That Old Black Magic' – to overcome what he saw as her inability to 'concentrate enough to sing the song to a playback, and then sing it for the camera by lip-synching'.

The song was done 'with two cameras, live, and with a hidden orchestra that was baffled by cardboard and canvas screens. With the two cameras Marilyn was free to perform the song as she wanted to . . .'

The result, says Logan, was 'a memorable musical sequence, primarily because we gave a great artist, a superb comedienne, the freedom to perform the way she felt'.

Paul Wurtzel, who worked on the 'Bus Stop' special effects when the crew returned to the studio from the Phoenix locations, remembers it as 'one of Marilyn's best films'. He remembers it, too, for the new snow machines that 'spewed out (soap) detergent for falling snow and almost took the paint off everything'. (The machines also gave Logan trouble; he spent the better part of one shooting day trying to figure out how to keep the machines from throwing out yellow-tinted 'snow'.)

Filming on 'Bus Stop' also stopped for several days when Marilyn contracted pneumonia and was hospitalized. Despite all the things that were going well for her in this period in which she was embarking on her own productions, her health problems seemed to be increasing. In addition, according to a number of persons who knew her best during these years, she had developed a pattern of increasing alcohol and drug abuse that was to have disastrous consequences.

As Lionel Newman recalls it, 'When I first got to work with her, she never drank; then came a time when she would drink a glass of wine . . . not drunk, (but) she would just have a glass of wine.'

But others remember a time when Marilyn would drink glass after glass of champagne during the day, and at night would take various types of sleeping pills.

Continued on page 177

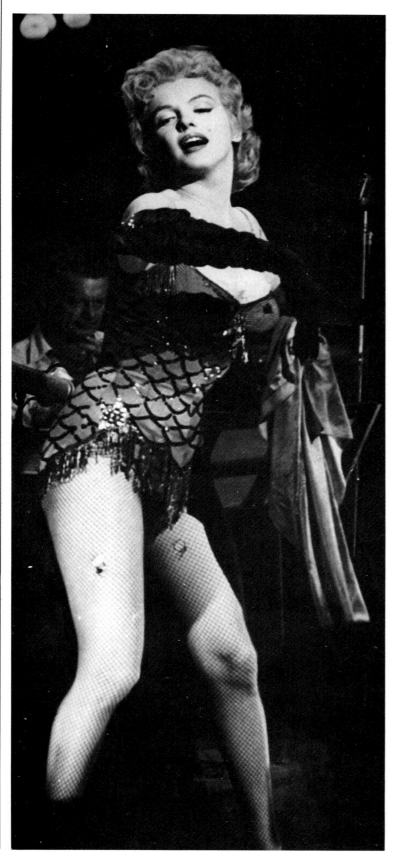

More than one person remembers the aftermath of her involvement with the vocal coach as the catalyst for her behaviour.

However, to Whitey Snyder, who had known her from her earliest film career, there was another, deeper cause:

'She was always worried about her sleep unrestfulness and so she'd go to bed real early – that's the trouble with pills; she'd go home and go to bed about seven-thirty and take a pill and wake up about an hour later and take another one, and wake up about midnight and take another one, and by six in the morning, she was dopey.

'I used to tell her a long, long time ago, "Goddamnit, you're going to screw up one day." And she did, a couple of times, but she'd gotten to the phone and they pumped her stomach (or) whatever they do . . .

'This last time – there are a lot of stories (about) how she died, and how she was murdered and all . . . I think she took an overdose of pills, was reaching across the bed for the phone and didn't make it.'

Let's Make Love/Something's Got To Give

What a long, long way Marilyn Monroe had come in the decade since first she had walked through that studio gate on Pico boulevard! And before her death at the age of thirty-six – seemingly on the very verge of the full flowering of her beauty and her powers – she would yet come a long way more.

After Josh Logan, these were the directors with whom she worked: Laurence Olivier; Billy Wilder; George Cukor; John Huston.

After 'Bus Stop', she completed four more films, of which only one – 'Let's Make Love' – was done on the Fox lot. That filming of 'Love', directed by George Cukor, caused a sensation as the 1950s gave way to a new decade, when the press ballyhooed an off-screen affair between herself and her co-star, Yves Montand.

Marilyn began a fifth picture – 'Something's Got to Give', also directed by Cukor and also shot on the Fox lot – but the production collapsed under the weight of delays, recriminations and lawsuits. Marilyn was fired from the picture and within two months was dead from a barbiturate overdose.

RIGHT (ABOVE AND BELOW): **Monroe and Yves Montand in 'Let's Make Love'.**
Both photographs copyright © Twentieth Century Fox Film Corporation

Why?

That question has echoed down the decades since August 1962, prompting everything from baroque conspiracy theories to learned Freudian analyses.

A definitive answer is probably impossible and likely it will remain so. However, there are facts and observations to set against the speculation.

Marilyn's personal life continued its wrenching rollercoaster course. The marriage to playwright Arthur Miller that began after 'Bus Stop' was over before 'Something's Got to Give'.

Her artistic aspirations continued to be boundless, but her opportunities were severely circumscribed. That universally remarked-upon nervous insecurity continued to hamper her efforts *and* her production schedules. Simply put, Marilyn Monroe had a life-long case of stage-fright and professional performance anxiety. Were forty takes on a four-word line worth the effort to reach perfection?

And then, of course, there were the excruciatingly complex business dealings of Marilyn Monroe, executive producer, to be set against the disdain that many in the Hollywood business community felt for the person they still regarded as a bubble-headed blonde. Drink and drugs must have seemed an easy answer to artistic pain and professional humiliation.

Still, her critical notices were never better and, even as the end approached, there were happy times too.

BELOW: One of the happy moments – Marilyn celebrates her birthday during the making of 'Something's Got To Give'.
Copyright © Twentieth Century Fox Film Corporation

'Don't say Hollywood killed Marilyn Monroe,' says Gene Allen, former president of the Academy of Motion Picture Arts and Sciences (the organization that each year presents the Academy Awards), and perhaps better known as the Oscar-winning art director of 'My Fair Lady'.

Allen was for a long time a member of George Cukor's professional family and worked on both of the Cukor/Marilyn sets. He joins a number of astute observers of Marilyn's final days who make the point that, far from destroying her, it was Hollywood that enabled her to carry on for as long as she did. In this view, it was the work and the acclaim in films that brought a measure of stability to an inherently frail personality.

'Let's Make Love' was the last time Lionel Newman worked with Marilyn. Even then, he remembers, 'she was nothing but a pro with us, the musicians,' and she found comfort in the picture's musical numbers. (Marilyn sang four songs in 'Let's Make Love', including Cole Porter's 'My Heart Belongs to Daddy'.

Newman emphasizes that he neither knew nor cared whether or not she and Montand had an affair during the filming of 'Love'. ('We were too busy working and it wasn't our business anyway,' he says simply.) And his respect and affection for Montand is plain.

Nonetheless, he remembers the press field-day over The Affair: Marilyn didn't seem to be as happy during that picture as on the others, he notes, pointing to the double standard of the day, which meant that Montand wasn't subject to moralistic press criticism and 'wasn't put down as much as Marilyn for what had happened'.

Whitey Snyder, among others, points to the irony in the fact that it was Arthur Miller who first suggested Montand for the part of the billionaire who falls for Marilyn. A number of observers of that time recall an aura of mutual respect that prevailed, despite their public difficulties, among Yves Montand and his wife, actress Simone Signoret, and Marilyn and Arthur Miller.

Apropos of the press inquisition that attended that filming, one observer on the set remarks that, 'When an actor and actress are up there kissing for twenty takes, there's an electricity in the air, whether anything's going on or not.'

Gene Allen first met Marilyn during the pre-production of the 'Let's Make Love' musical numbers. His initial impression was of a girl who was 'nice, giggly, sweet and lovable'.

Once again Jack Cole was Marilyn's choreographer. Allen recalls that during the actual filming of Marilyn's musical numbers, Cole would stand right alongside the camera and do an exact, in-time, mirror-image rendition of each movement of the dance; and, while Marilyn seemed to be looking into the camera as she danced, in reality she was following along with her choreographer.

During the filming of one number, Allen stood on one side of the camera, watching Marilyn, while Jack danced on the other. Suddenly, much to Allen's shock, Marilyn in mid-dance grimaced and clutched her chest!

Was it an attack of some sort? No, it was Jack Cole's foot caught in a dolly track and run over by the camera. Perfect-student Marilyn had automatically followed suit after her teacher's unexpected movements!

Between 'Let's Make Love' and the fiasco of 'Something's Got to Give', the last two years of Marilyn's life elapsed. Allen recalls that Marilyn 'had lost a lot of weight and looked terrific' on the latter set (which, incidentally, was an exact replica of George Cukor's real-life home).

Continued on page 188

When he viewed the dailies of her early scenes, however, says Allen, there was an apparent on-screen difference between the Marilyn of 'Love' and the Marilyn of 'Give', who showed a 'vagueness' and 'indecision' in playing her scenes. 'It became apparent to everyone who saw the rushes that there was a problem,' he adds.

Although her drug and alcohol use doubtless contributed to that 'problem', Marilyn at the time also was suffering from a lingering pneumonia-like infection, which, according to Whitey, was aggravated by her lengthy swimming-pool scene.

As her bad health and bad nerves caused increasing delays, studio officials became increasingly anxious.

More than one analyst of that Hollywood period has pointed to the multi-million-dollar budget overruns that the studio then was experiencing on 'Cleopatra' – which threatened for a time to topple the entire studio into bankruptcy – as a reason for that heightened anxiety. *Continued on page 208*

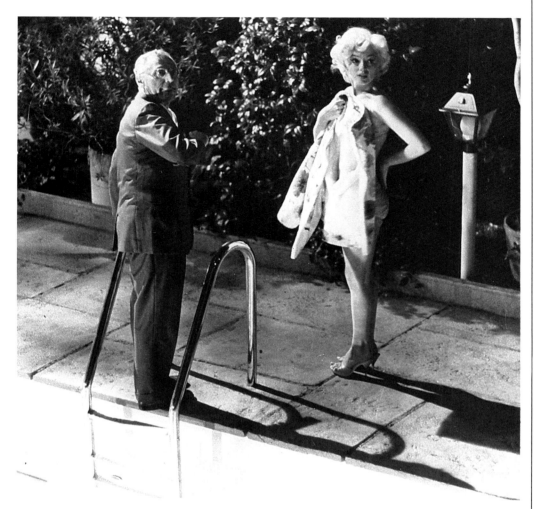

PAGES 186 AND 187: Going, going, gone! Marilyn models one of her costumes for 'Something's Got To Give'.
All copyright © Twentieth Century Fox Film Corporation

PAGES 188 TO 195: On the set of the swimming pool scene from 'Something's Got To Give'. George Cukor was the director of the film, which also starred Dean Martin.
All pictures copyright © Twentieth Century Fox Film Corporation

PAGES 196 TO 209 INCLUSIVE: A selection of photographs of Marilyn on the set of 'Something's Got To Give'. Gene Allen, former president of the Academy of Motion Picture Arts and Sciences, recalled that Marilyn 'had lost a lot of weight and looked terrific' on the set, but when he viewed the 'dailies' of her early scenes there was an apparent on-screen difference between the Marilyn of 'Love' and the Marilyn of 'Give', who showed a 'vagueness' and 'indecision' in playing her scenes.
All photographs copyright © Twentieth Century Fox Film Corporation

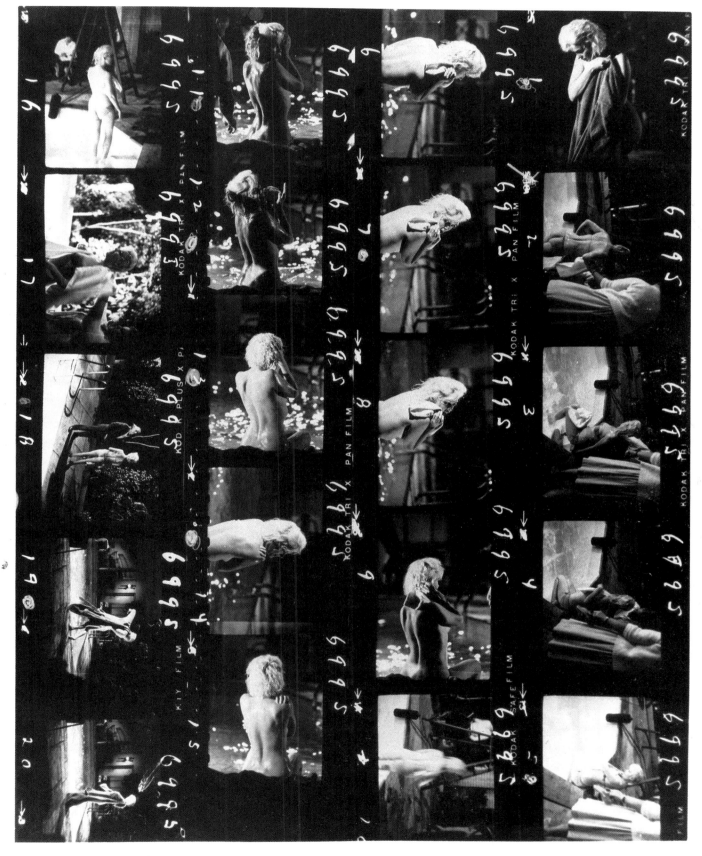

LADIES
WARDROBE

PICTURE A-855 Date 4·30·62
TITLE Somethings Got To Give
DIRECTOR G. CUKOR
ACTRESS M. MONROE
PART OF ELLEN
CHANGE No. #4
EXT. ARDEN HOME
Sc 82
SCENE No.
Designer J. LOUIS 8x10

ABOVE: Marilyn gets a present from director,
George Cukor.

Allen says flatly that, despite the delays, George Cukor was prepared to continue the shoot.

Paul Wurtzel, who also was on that set, remembers that the crew – despite negative publicity at the time – remained sympathetic to Marilyn's troubles. And when Marilyn was dismissed, she sent the cast and crew a telegram saying that what had happened was not her fault.

Publicist Johnny Campbell, who also was there, recalls that the escalating problems on the set prompted him to begin a daily log of events in which he recorded the facts of the ever-building tensions.

When Marilyn was fired, shortly after her birthday party on the set, her co-star Dean Martin resigned from the cast in protest. Lawyers swung into action.

In the final two months of Marilyn's life, much of the 'Something's Got to Give' tempest was brought to a business-like, perhaps even an amicable, resolution. Shooting of the picture was set to resume in September with both Dean *and* Marilyn.

But the happy ending was not to be. Marilyn Monroe died early in August 1962. And Whitey Snyder, who had applied Marilyn's make-up in her first screen test, had one more task to perform. He says:

'Way back to "Gentlemen Prefer Blondes" she was . . . in hospital . . .

'When she was going to get out . . . naturally I went over there to make her up, so when she met the public or the press or anybody she'd look alright. So I did; I put the make-up on before she went out.

'At that time she says, "Will you promise me that if something happens to me in this world, when I die or anything like that, promise me you'll do my make-up, so I look good when I leave?"

'And I says, "Sure, bring the body back while it's warm."

'Well, I still have this money clip she gave me at the end of "Gentlemen Prefer Blondes" that says, "Whitey, dear. While I'm still warm. Marilyn."

'It was a gag at that time.

'So, when she died Joe (DiMaggio) called me from New York and said, "Whitey, you promised." They all knew about the money clip.

'I said, "Okay", and I did it. I went down to Westwood (to the mortuary) . . .

'There she was on an iron table. I had to go over and grab her right away, put my hand on her head. I'm a coward and I would've run down the street, but I touched her and it was alright.

'(And) it didn't bother me making her up when she was laying down, because I did it so many times with her on location . . .'

And so Marilyn Monroe was dead. But the legend lives on.

Afterword

Marilyn Monroe's quips were made up by the Twentieth Century Fox publicity department . . . or were they? And, as everyone knew, Roy Craft was the one who made them up . . . but did he?

Craft denies it. She made up all her famous lines, he says.

Some examples of the wit and wisdom of Marilyn Monroe:

What did Marilyn have on during the shooting of her infamous calendar? 'The radio.'

What did she wear to bed? 'Chanel Number Five.'

Only Chanel Number Five? 'I like to wear something different once in a while. Now and then I switch to Arpège.'

Why didn't Marilyn have a tan? 'Because I like to feel blonde all over.'

Had anyone ever accused her of wearing falsies? 'My answer to that is, quote: Those who know me better, know better. That's all. Unquote.'

Did the screen's most famous sex symbol have any love interests of her own? 'No serious interests, but I'm always interested.'

When asked to compare Hollywood's preoccupation with sex with the rest of the country, she replied, 'I haven't taken a sexus – I mean a census – but sex is sex and that's good, isn't it?'

She described her fur coat as 'Fox – and not the Twentieth Century kind.'

When asked how long she'd had her distinctive walk, Marilyn replied 'I started when I was six months old and haven't stopped yet.'

To a crowd of screaming marines, she chided 'You fellows down there are always whistling at sweater girls. Well, you take away their sweaters and what have you got?'

She also dismissed sweater girls as having just 'a couple of things' in their favour.

When Japanese journalists asked Marilyn if it was true that she wore nothing under her dress, she replied, 'I'm planning to buy a kimono tomorrow.'

Why did the beautiful Marilyn want to do the *Brothers Karamazov*? 'I don't want to play the *brothers*. I want to play Grushenka from that book. She's a girl.'

When asked about her bedroom voice, Marilyn quipped '*Bedroom* voice? I use this voice everywhere, except in the bedroom.' And poignantly she explained, 'I live alone.'

TEXT ACKNOWLEDGEMENTS

The Publishers wish to acknowledge the following for the reproduction of quotations from their publications in this book:

Betty Grable: The Reluctant Movie Queen by Doug Warren, published by St Martin's Press Inc, New York, in USA and Canada, and Robson Books, London, in British Commonwealth excluding Canada. Copyright © by Doug Warren.

Intermission by Anne Baxter, published by G. P. Putnam, New York, in USA and Canada, and Angus & Robertson, London, in British Commonwealth excluding Canada. Copyright © 1976 by Anne Baxter.

Movie Stars, Real People and Me by Joshua L. Logan, reprinted by permission of Delacorte Press, New York. Copyright © 1978 by Joshua L. Logan.

Shelley: Also Known as Shirley by Shelley Winters, reprinted by permission of Grafton Books, a Division of the Collins Publishing Group. Copyright © 1980 by Shelley Winters.

American Weekly, 23 November 1952, article by Liza Wilson.

Colliers magazine.

Movie Spotlight, April 1954, article by Earl Leaf.